RECORD MAN

The story of Phil Gernhard, Florida's Nº 1 hit producer

Bill DeYoung

Revised and expanded edition

Originally published in 2018 by University Press of Florida under the title of
Phil Gernhard, Record Man by Bill DeYoung
ISBN 978-0-813056-77-7
Revised and Expanded Edition
Copyright ©2024

Published by St. Petersburg Press
St. Petersburg, FL
www.stpetersburgpress.com

Design and composition by St. Petersburg Press
Cover design by St. Petersburg Press and Isa Crosta
Cover photo by Deborah Triplett
Back cover image: Laurie Records

Print ISBN: 978-1-964239-08-8

"Gernhard's production quantity may be less than other leading producers, but his scoring percentage is among the best."

Billboard
Dec. 21, 1968

"One of Phil's flaws: He read a couple of books that must've been written by somebody like Donald Trump. They told him 'The way to riches is never pay anybody for anything.'"

Dick Holler
Oct. 6, 2016

"Phil was a producer, a publisher, a promoter — a total record man. Maybe I've met five in my lifetime. He was one of them."

Mike Curb
Oct. 20, 2016

For Jack and Annie

Contents

SNOOPY versus
THE RED BARON

Words and Music by P. GERNHARD and D. HOLLER

Recorded by THE ROYAL GUARDSMEN on Laurie Records

KEYS
04901

SANPHIL MUSIC PUB.

Foreword

Phil Gernhard is one of the most important Floridians in the history of popular music.

Even if they've never heard his name, most people know one or two of the songs he produced and made famous, from "Snoopy vs. the Red Baron" to "Abraham, Martin and John," from "Me and You and a Dog Named Boo" to "Let Your Love Flow."

On a professional level, he was a gifted record-maker who often boasted that he had "golden ears" and knew a hit song the first time he heard it.

He was also a hustler whose insistence on looking out for No. 1 (Phil Gernhard) resulted in animus, broken contracts and lawsuits. Despite his many triumphs, Gernhard left a legacy of bad blood and lasting hostility.

His personal demons, including a toxic relationship with his abusive father, four failed marriages and addictions to booze and pills, ensured that he would never be able to fully enjoy his success.

Yet Gernhard's contributions to music, and to the State of Florida, should forever be celebrated.

Bill DeYoung
May 2024

(This book is a revised and expanded edition of Phil Gernhard Record Man, *published in 2018 by University Press of Florida.)*

Phil Gernhard and Betty Vernon, Thanksgiving 2007 at the Vernon home in Bradenton. "He was dying, he had no family and he wanted to leave his estate to me. I knew he had made it big in the music industry, but that's all I knew." Photo: Jim Vernon.

Rosebud

The ghost of a man standing in Betty Vernon's doorway grinned at her under dark and deep-set eyes. *Skin and bones*, she thought, sizing him up. *Jeez*.

She hadn't expected it to be this bad. He looked, she'd remember later, like *death on a cracker*.

Still, Betty smiled at her hollow-cheeked visitor and decided to make the best of it. When he broke the ice, blurting out "You're so skinny!," she smiled and replied "Look who's talking!" Then she hugged him, half expecting him to snap in two, and invited him inside.

Phil Gernhard had been her very first sweetheart, in the mid 1950s. She was Elizabeth Van Doninck then, an eighth grader at St. Martha's Catholic School in Sarasota, Florida. Phil was older, a sophomore at Sarasota High.

Nearly 50 years later, he'd accepted a Thanksgiving invitation to her modest home in Bradenton, just a few miles from where they'd both grown up. The house she shared with her husband of four decades, Jim. The house that filled up with boisterous children, grandchildren and great-grandchildren on holidays.

Gernhard had driven straight through to Bradenton from his big brick house in Brentwood, one of Nashville's most exclusive suburbs, loading an overnight bag into the back of his giant black Humvee for the 12-hour drive south.

The Humvee was a trophy car, the kind driven by wealthy men who are used to riding high and looking down on the rest of the world, and envied by those who drove smaller and less imposing vehicles.

He'd filled his house, and his life, with such possessions, because he was rich, and he enjoyed status symbols. Phil Gernhard was, on that Thanksgiving weekend in 2007, a successful executive in the music industry, a man who not only influenced popular culture in America, but helped to plan things and carefully make them happen. In every sense, Phil Gernhard was a player.

For three decades, he'd been the key man on the A&R (Artists and Repertoire) team at Nashville-based Curb Records, where he'd molded, advised and worked tirelessly for such country stars as Tim McGraw, Jo Dee Messina and Rodney Atkins, making sure they had just the right songs, recorded with the right producers, and had those songs played on the right radio stations. Without him, none of them would have made a ripple.

He'd started young. As a 19-year-old college student, away at the University of South Carolina, Gernhard — entirely untrained in music-making but never a fan of sitting in class - had produced a handful of singles for the rhythm 'n' blues singing group Maurice Williams and the Zodiacs. The third of these, the Williams-penned "Stay," was issued on a national label and went to No. 1 on the charts. It sold more than a million copies.

Back in Florida, he then co-wrote the novelty hit "Snoopy vs. the Red Baron," America's fastest-selling single of 1966. It had been Gernhard who "found" the teen garage band the Royal Guardsmen and produced a string of "Snoopy" singles for them throughout the decade, negotiating a royalty deal with cartoonist Charles M. Schulz, creator of the comic strip beagle.

"Snoopy vs. the Red Baron" sold five million records around the world.

After the novelty wore off and the public abandoned the Guardsmen, Gernhard did, too, only to revive the sagging career of one-time doo-wop singer Dion DiMucci with a maudlin ballad called "Abraham, Martin and John." Another million seller.

Gernhard then discovered and produced hit records for his fellow Floridians Lobo ("Me and You and a Dog Named Boo," "I'd Love You to Want Me"), Jim Stafford ("Spiders and Snakes," "Wildwood Weed") and the Bellamy Brothers ("Let Your Love Flow").

Phil Gernhard was a legend.

Until he threw in his lot with Curb, he'd been entirely independent. In the 1960s and into the '70s, independent producers found the talent, produced the records and sold the final product — a finished master recording — to the highest bidder. They paid the production costs up front, but if a record hit, the money came rolling in, especially if the next record by the same artist sold well, too. Then all the terms were re-negotiated accordingly, the distributing label more than willing to share the wealth with an independent who reliably brought them hits.

It happened with the Royal Guardsmen and Laurie Records, with Lobo at Big Tree, and with Stafford at MGM. All Florida artists, discovered and developed by Phil Gernhard. Multiple hits, bigger paychecks each time.

Gernhard was a self-made man, but he didn't get rich by being stupid. In his production deals, he almost always negotiated a piece of the song's publishing for himself — sometimes more than that.

Which meant that he not only got paid for producing the record, and for delivering the record to the label, he got paid — in part - for the songs themselves, songs he had no hand in composing.

This was fairly common practice at the time, and some recording artists considered it part of their deal with the devil — after all, Gernhard worked extremely hard on their behalf.

Others didn't take it so well.

Betty Vernon didn't know any of this until she'd received a phone call, out of the blue, in the fall of 2007, from a woman who identified herself as a private investigator. "If you're Elizabeth Vernon," the voice said mysteriously, "someone wants to give you something."

A practical, no-nonsense woman, Vernon smelled a scam, the kind of thing senior Floridians often fall prey to. She hung up, and the woman called back repeatedly over the following days. Finally, Vernon challenged her: "If you're on the up and up, and this isn't a scam, then you won't mind meeting me in my attorney's office."

The woman agreed, but at the arranged meeting she hemmed and hawed and wouldn't divulge her client's name, saying he wished to remain anonymous. Still skeptical, Vernon pressed her. The private investigator pulled out her phone and placed a call. "Unless I give Mrs. Vernon your name, she's not talking to me," she said.

The call ended, and there was a long pause before the woman spoke.

"She finally said it was Phil. He was dying, he had no family and he wanted to leave his estate to me," Vernon explained. "I knew he had made it big in the music industry, but that's all I knew."

Phil Gernhard. The skinny, red-haired kid with the adorable gap between his front teeth, who rode Schwinn bikes and the city bus with her everywhere in those sunny, halcyon days. The boy who sat in the back seat of her mom's car, chattering away, while Mrs. Van Doninck drove her daughter to Lido Beach for crack-of-dawn summertime swim practice.

Her first sweetheart.

"He always worked," Vernon remembered. "He told me he had a paper route when he was a kid, and it got so big he had sub-divided it with other kids. He had a little business going. That young, he was already an entrepreneur."

As a teenager, "he had a job working in the kitchen in one of the big department store restaurants downtown, and when a new Elvis record hit, he had it and he was back at my house and we were dancing. They were happy times."

Sitting in the conference room of her lawyer's office, Vernon stared at Gernhard's emissary with disbelief.

"She said 'Do you remember the Sadie Hawkins Dance?' In those days, girls didn't ask boys out, except on Sadie Hawkins Day. I had invited him. She told me Phil said that was the happiest day of his life."

Wow, Betty thought. *That's kind of pathetic.* It was a lot for her to take in.

She remembered that she had heard from Gernhard exactly once in all the years gone by, rather indirectly. In August 1977, the day Elvis Presley died, "I got a telegram — no return address, no nothing. And all it said was 'Part of our youth has died. Phil.'"

She asked for, and got, Gernhard's email address, and wrote to him. At first shy and tentative, their correspondence led to a series of increasingly lengthy phone calls. "Fifty years of catching up," they called it.

He told her he had cancer, and that his doctor had said he wouldn't live to see the year 2010. He was putting his entire life — his decisions, the good and the bad — under a microscope. He told Betty she was the only girl he'd ever loved.

"He had a beautiful home, in a high-end neighborhood," she said. "He told me 'I was sitting there thinking what am I gonna do with all this?' He had no children. He said 'I'm gonna give it to Betty.' That came to his brain.

"He wanted to leave me his estate, and he wanted to set up a college trust fund for all my grandchildren."

How did he know all about her? "I guess the private investigator had poked around and earned her money."

Jim Vernon, a retired civil engineer, was Betty's second husband. Phil told her Jim was a lucky guy. "He wanted to know about my grandchildren," she explained. "He wanted to know about Jim. And what happened with my first marriage."

Gernhard, who had been married four times, and was at that moment well into a protracted, bitter divorce, told his old flame that he'd only tied the knot once, and that it hadn't ended well. And he left it vague. "Maybe he didn't want me to think ill of him — married, divorced, married, divorced, married, divorced," Vernon said.

She didn't question anything he told her.

She asked Phil about celebrities she thought a lot of; he'd met pretty much all of them, and was hard to impress. Still, he thrilled her with inside-baseball stories.

"He told me how insane it was in the '70s in California. The affluence and the corruption in the business. The drugs. He said it was like a buffet — the drugs were out on the table, whatever you wanted. He was very upfront about it. And he lost so many friends when the AIDS epidemic hit."

He told her about the artists he'd worked with, how his particular talent was matching the right song with the right performer. He told her about Mike Curb, the CEO of his record company, and how they'd been friends since the 1970s. Curb Records was almost exclusively a country music label, unlike the music they'd danced to in their youth. Phil didn't produce any more, but his ears were golden. He would be an asset to any record company. He liked Curb.

He talked about everything except his illness. He struck her as a very,

very lonely man looking back on a life of disappointments and missed opportunities. He'd given every bit of himself to music.

"He says to me one day 'What do you want? What do you need?' I had no idea what he was thinking. I said 'Well, my car is nine years old.' Then he said 'Where do you like to travel?' I said 'I'd love to go to Alaska, and I've always wanted to drive down the Pacific Coast Highway.'"

Soon, a chocolate-brown 2008 GMC Acadia was delivered to the Vernons' driveway. He also made arrangements to send Betty and Jim on an Alaskan cruise, first class all the way, then travel to California by train where they'd drive a rental car south on the scenic PCH and fly back to Florida out of Los Angeles.

Gernhard's Thanksgiving visit to the Vernons' house was the first time he'd been back since his mother's funeral, 12 years before. Then, he'd clashed with his father and vowed never to return.

Something — maybe it was cancer - changed his mind.

He took a suite in the Sarasota Ritz-Carlton, just two blocks from the Episcopal church he'd attended with his family in the '40s and '50s. Betty and Jim stood with him on the ornate balcony, overlooking the harbor and the Gulf of Mexico, and he sighed as he said "I forgot how beautiful Florida is." They all went out to dinner.

More than 20 people crowded into the Vernon home for Thanksgiving, and Gernhard — dressed all in black and never removing his yellow-tinted sunglasses - surprised her hosts by acting sociable and making polite conversation with everyone, even the children.

"But he was really sick," Betty said. "Every once in a while he'd say 'Excuse me,' and go off to the bathroom to take medicine." He had to step outside when the banquet was laid out on the dining room table — Betty thought the smell was turning his stomach.

When a Vernon family friend, a doctor, asked him what kind of cancer it was, Gernhard snapped 'I don't want to talk about it.'"

He did enjoy talking about his "Girl Friday," a Curb employee named Kelly Lynn. "It was 'Kelly, Kelly, Kelly.' She took care of him. She was almost like a mother figure. He had a little fanny pack thing because he was taking all kinds of drugs. He was very ill. He said 'Kelly fixed me up here, and I'm all set. I can't function without Kelly.' He thought the world of her. He was paying for her son to go to a private school.

"There were times you could tell his brain wasn't functioning correctly, and I think that's what pushed him over the edge. He didn't want to be like that. And he was going deaf. Mike Curb had said to him, 'For God's sake, Phil. Of all people, you can't go deaf.'"

Before he left town, he showed the Vernons photos from his recent vacation to Scotland. There was no one else in the pictures; he'd gone alone. That, too, struck Betty as exceptionally sad.

The holiday over, Gernhard returned to his Brentwood estate, to Curb Records and to his Girl Friday. The visit, Mike Curb would say later, "brought him tremendous closure. He explained it to my wife and I ... There was even a spiritual aspect to it that he didn't speak too much about, but since he had never spoken about spiritual things before, it was very interesting to hear him talk about that aspect of life."

He and Betty still spoke on the phone, but less frequently, and she could tell he was getting weaker. He would sometimes just stop talking in the middle of a sentence, his mind wandering, or searching for something intangible ... or just going blank as the disease, or whatever it was, ravaged it.

As 2007 turned into 2008, she still had difficulty processing what had happened. "It was crazy; it was insane," Vernon said. "My husband and my kids knew, but I didn't tell anybody else because it was so wacky. It was a long time before I said anything to anybody about it."

Betty worried about her strange, emaciated, troubled friend.

By mid-February, she hadn't heard from him in weeks. She feared the worst.

On the 22nd, she received a call from Steve Parker, Gernhard's accountant and the designated executor of his will. Phil had been found dead on his bedroom floor; he'd put the barrel of a silver revolver in his mouth and pulled the trigger.

Parker wanted to talk about his bequests to Betty and her family.

He had everything, and he had nothing.

It's tempting to dismiss Phil Gernhard as some self-medicating Charles Foster Kane, a used-up old man wandering the lonely rooms of his cavernous Tennessee Xanadu, surrounded by his trophies and awards and the possessions he never got around to uncrating.

Yet the fictional Kane focused his considerable talent, ego and ambition on little more than the edification and glorification of Charles Foster Kane.

Although he certainly enjoyed the money, and the notoriety, Gernhard's focus was almost always on channeling *his* considerable talent, ego and ambition to seed the success of others.

Still, like Kane he died alone, inside a cocoon of his own making, thinking back to happier days, to an innocent time when he knew how to love, and be loved, without suspicion or judgement.

2

All Shook Up

When Phil Gernhard, age 8, leaves today for Camp St. Andrew at Avon Park, he takes with him a man-sized black eye. He came by it out on the diamond at Payne Park where he was playing right field on a Little League team. In the third inning Phil caught a line drive with his left eye instead of his glove and had to be hustled away to the hospital, where he spent most of his time crying that he wanted to go back and finish the game.

"Main Street Reporter"
Sarasota Herald-Tribune
July 17, 1949

In Boyd Rains Gernhard's mind, there were two ways to do something: His way and the wrong way. Born in 1908 to German parents in Port Clinton, Ohio, a fishing town on the southwestern shore of Lake Erie, Boyd — whose nickname since childhood was "Bud" — learned stubbornness and the art of shouting others down from his father, who'd divorced his mother and moved out.

He liked his stepfather well enough, but he had a prickly relationship with Dad. Somehow, no matter how hard he worked at something, it was never good enough for the old man. For most of Boyd Gernhard's adult life, he and his father were estranged. In the early 1930s he graduated from Miami Military Institute, a strict step 'n' salute high school in Germantown, Ohio, and then enrolled at the University of Michigan, where he was in the same graduating class as future football legend Tom Harmon.

Bud Gernhard met and married Sara Arnold, from Shaker Heights, in 1935. Sara came from a family of means, and had aspired to a career as an artist (later in life, she confessed that she'd never gotten over her "one true love" from her Ohio days, the actor Jim Backus, who'd later be known for playing Thurston Howell III on TV's *Gilligan's Island*). Sara had manners; she was as cultured as her husband was crude.

Their daughter Judith Mae was born in the spring of 1939; a son, Phillip Arnold, arrived 20 months later, on Feb. 5, 1941.

When Phil was born, the family was living in Evanston, Ill., a Chicago suburb. His father was the regional distributor for Pabst Blue Ribbon and other favorite Midwestern beers. He was responsible for the introduction, in that area, of Baltimore-brewed National Bohemian beer, soon to be a national favorite.

America's entry into World War II turned the Gernhard family's world upside down, as it would so many millions of others. Boyd entered the Navy, and by 1944, because of his military education, he was a lieutenant running an advance base unit in Australia.

Before the war, he and Sara had enjoyed a winter vacation trip to Anna Maria Island, a sparsely-inhabited barrier island near Sarasota on Florida's west coast. Desperate to get his family out of the Midwest, with its long, cold winters and its big-city nightmares, in late 1943 — Phil was not yet three years old - Boyd took out a lease on a small house near the beach and informed Sara that she and the kids were to wait for him there. When the war in the South Pacific finally ended, he would join them and they'd resume their lives together.

First, there were hurdles to get over. "You couldn't get metal parts or rubber during the war," remembered Judee Gernhard, Phil's sister. "But my grandfather, Phil Arnold, was vice president of the Garlock Packing Company — they packed up machinery parts for shipment overseas.

"We had an old Chevy called Tokyo Rose, and her floorboards were all rusted out, so we had wooden floorboards. But my grandfather was able to get tires for her. So my mother, brother and I, and our big boxer dog, Regent, drove to Florida."

On Oct. 19, 1944, a Category 4 hurricane made landfall at Sarasota. Residents of Anna Maria Island, including the Gernhard family, were evacuated to higher ground. "We lived on the far side of the island, away from the Gulf of Mexico," said Judee. "And there were houses across the street, right on the Gulf.

"When we came back, after the storm, our house was still standing. But all of the houses on the Gulf side had washed away. They were just gone.

"There was a water heater on our back porch, and my mother kept dishcloths hanging on nails back there. And when we came back, the dishcloths were all still there, but every house across the street was gone. I remember thinking how strange that was."

Once the war ended, Boyd arrived in Florida to pick up where he'd left off. He landed a job as a traveling salesman. And he got involved in the community, co-founding the Sarasota Young Republicans Club in 1948. Boyd was the first president of the Sarasota Republican Party League, Florida's largest Republican action group of the era.

Sarasota County in that time was sleepy and relatively isolated, surrounded on three sides by cattle ranches and citrus groves. The Interstate highway system didn't come that far south, so tourists weren't exactly arriving by the busload.

The population in 1950 was just under 29,000, and although the number would triple within a decade, it would be years before the area became a winter playground for rich northerners, and a retirement destination for the moneyed from all over the world.

Midwestern circus king John Ringling and his wife Mable, however, had wintered in the city since the early days of the 20th century, and in 1926 moved into "Ca' d'Zan," an ornate palace built to their specifications, in Venetian Gothic style, on the edge of the Gulf of Mexico.

In an area with virtually no wealth, and especially during the Great Depression, the Ringlings were particularly ostentatious. They constructed an enormous art museum on the grounds, replete with faux-Roman statuary standing guard over an ornamental garden, to house their vast collection of European art.

Ringling died in 1936, outliving his wife by seven years. He willed the home, and the art museum, to the City of Sarasota. It was virtually ignored by the locals, who saw it every day as they drove up and down Tamiami Trail, the city's main artery.

What Sarasota — the county and the city — had going for it was the Gulf, beautiful and blue and, in the '50s, relatively undeveloped. If you were a kid in Sarasota, you went to the beach. That was the very definition of fun and recreation.

When Judee and Phil Gernhard were growing up, the city was fully segregated, with the black population living in an impoverished area known as Newtown. The "black beach" was nearly 40 miles away from Sarasota, near the Venice airport.

Phil Gernhard, Sarasota High School senior. Family photo.

The Gernhards lived in several different homes before settling into a roomy, ranch-style place on Bayshore Road, almost directly across the street from Sarasota Jungle Gardens, the city's lone tourist destination, a carbon copy of Tampa's Busch Gardens, and Sunken Gardens in St. Petersburg.

The kids grew up with the incessant, nail-biting sound of screeching parrots, and the sight of colorful flamingos and peacocks — gone AWOL from Jungle Gardens — stalking across their front yard and making a mess of things.

But the biggest danger was impossible to ignore. Boyd Gernhard was an alcoholic, and prone to blindsiding his wife and children with what Judee called "rage-aholic fits." If things weren't exactly as Boyd wanted them, he'd get abusive, first verbally, and then physically. The children were terrified of him.

"He was out on the road a lot," Judee remembered. "And Mommy and Phil and I, and our dog, would just kind of live like we normally lived Monday through Thursday. And come Friday, we had to have the house all cleaned up. We couldn't sit in the chairs. We couldn't make dents in the pillows. It was pretty scary. I don't think he was bi-polar -nobody knew what that was then - but he also had a wonderful sense of humor and was very charismatic. But he really ruled the roost."

When things got especially bad, the Gernhard kids would run away to the John and Mable Ringling Museum of Art, nearly a mile away, and hide in the spacious Roman gardens, among the fountains and statuary. There, they'd whisper to one another, their eyes darting furtively from one entranceway to the next, wondering if their mother would come and find them, and explain that everything would be better now.

She never did.

"My father was very abusive to my mother and me, and Phil would try to stand up to him," Judee said. "Phil determined at an early age that he was going to make a lot of money, and go back and rescue my mother. Get her out of there. And he did, and he tried, and she wouldn't leave, and he was just completely heartbroken."

Phil's buddy George Heiland saw up close the fear that Boyd Gernhard had instilled in his son. As Sarasota High seniors, they once attempted to take George's 12-foot motorboat across the bay for an overnight campout on Longboat Key.

The night was foggy and the boys putted along, with their 7½ horsepower outboard, and never found Longboat Key. Instead they drifted and fretted, and fitfully slept until their little craft was spotted in New Pass Inlet.

Following their rescue, a news photographer from the *Sarasota Herald-Tribune* approached Heiland on the dock. Before the man could take the photo, Gernhard made himself scarce. "He didn't want his dad to know he was out there with me," said Heiland. The next day's paper included a short piece about teenaged George Heiland's overnight boating mishap, with no mention of his companion.

The Heilands and the Van Donincks lived around the corner from the Gernhards. "We were part of the same neighborhood," Betty Vernon said. "All the kids that lived in the north end of Sarasota knew each other better than the kids from Siesta Key or South Sarasota. All my friends were from the north end."

But Phil and Betty's romance ended at the Gernhard front door. "I had dinner at his house just once," she recalled. "His mother used an electric mixer on the mashed potatoes, that's what I remember.

"After we re-connected, I said 'You know, I only had dinner at your house that one time.' Phil said 'My dad was ogling you. That's why I didn't want you to come back.' There was no love lost there at all."

Judy Gernhard, Sarasota High School's talented drum major, is the latest entry in the Sarasota Herald Tribune's Annual Miss Mail-Away Contest. Daughter of Mr. and Mrs. Boyd R. Gernhard of 3926 Bayshore Road, the high-stepping marcher weighs 132 pounds and measures 37-24-37.

"Judy Gernhard enters 'Cover Girl' Contest"
Sarasota Herald Tribune
Sept. 27, 1955

"In high school, I came along a year behind Judy and my teachers wouldn't let me forget that she was the good student."

Phil Gernhard
Sarasota Herald-Tribune
Sept. 3, 1988

"Phil was kind of quiet and introspective," recalled Sandy Gernhard, his future wife, "and Judee did everything right."

While eight-year-old Phil was away at Camp St. Andrew, nursing his black eye, Judy and her mother flew out for a ten-day vacation to Ohio — to visit Mrs. Gernhard's father, Phil's namesake — and then to New York City, where they took in a couple of Broadway shows and sat in the audience of a nationally-broadcast radio quiz show. Boyd, meanwhile, was on the road.

Teenage Judee took piano lessons and aspired to a career in music; Phil tried the trumpet for a while but gave up, then played the drums but was, by his own admission, not very good.

He just loved music — and records. "In junior high and high school, he was not a playing musician — he was a listening musician," Judee explained. "He just had an interest in the sounds that were coming out. He liked to dance and was very rhythmic."

On Feb. 21, 1956, Gernhard plunked down 50 cents of his hard-earned money, from working in a downtown cafeteria, to see his idol, Elvis Presley, at the Florida Theatre in Sarasota.

Presley played four shows at the theater that day. Betty Van Doninck attended one of them with her parents, before she and Phil started going out. They'd never heard of the performer before, and went out of curiosity.

Also on the bill: Justin Tubb, the Louvin Brothers and the Carter Sisters.

But Phil Gernhard only had eyes — and ears — for Elvis, who had just released "Heartbreak Hotel" in January.

"That night had a tremendous impact on my life and became a driving force in all these years as a record producer," Phil told the *Herald-Tribune* in 1988. "There's not a gold record or award on my wall that does not owe at least part of its existence to that night and the inspiration of his performance and personality."

This, most likely, represented the point of no return for Phil Gernhard. Thrilled and inspired by the blood rush of tangible excitement at the Elvis show, and otherwise intrigued by how music was created and recorded sounds assembled, he began to inwardly reject his father's hardline attitudes and stern dictums.

Boyd expected his son to follow in his footsteps and join the Navy. After all, it made a man out of the father — why not the son? "Phil never aspired to be in the military," Judee said. "We sort of skirted around those issues because my father was German — my way or the highway."

But pleasing Dad was always in the back of Phil's mind. Even though he felt a strong pull from a very different direction, he tried, time and again, to toe the family line. In his senior year at Sarasota High School, he joined the Naval ROTC and learned to march and sweat (he already knew how to take orders).

After graduation and a summer job at a lumber yard, he left Sarasota for the University of South Carolina, where he would be enrolled in undergraduate studies as a midshipman in the Naval Reserve Officer Training Corps.

At USC, his declared major was naval science. He was one of 20 "midshipmen" given an extensive tour of Pensacola Naval Air Station, one of the perks of the naval science program at USC.

"He loved being in South Carolina," said Judee, who was away in Tallahassee, studying music at Florida State University. "He really found his niche there."

Back in Sarasota, the old man was fuming.

Judee: "Our roads didn't cross, except when we were both at home. I was on the one path, 'gonna get good grades and graduate' and do everything Mommy and Daddy wanted me to do, and he was kinda like 'I'm outta here. I'm gonna do this, and I'm gonna do that, and then I'm gonna do the other thing.' But he was very talented. And very charismatic."

Phil's four years in Columbia, S.C. — with only the first actually spent in school — would change everything. "There was a whole different part of his personality that was already coloring outside the lines," his sister added. "His heart was always someplace other than where my father wanted his feet to be."

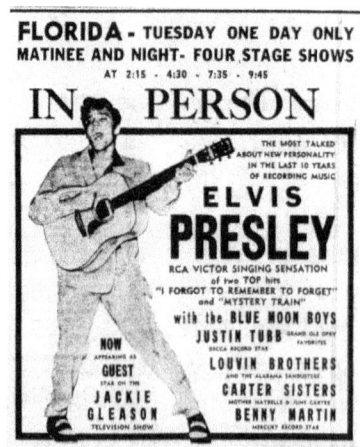

③

Oh Won't You Stay

Vincent Cole and Phil Bernhard (sic) have formed Cole Records in Columbia, S.C. Artists on Cole are Maurice Williams, the Zodiacs and the Royal Sultans.

Billboard
"Music As Written"
Aug. 24, 1959

Johnny McCullough was a songwriter, a piano player and a man on the move; he liked to drink, and he liked to laugh. In 1959 the fun-loving Florida native was in Nashville, gigging on the legendary Printers Alley and trying to place songs with somebody who might record them and make him rich. "I heard people talking about production," he recalled. "So I asked what a producer was, and they told me. And I said 'I can do that.'"

Soon McCullough and his older brother Jimmy had landed in Columbia. "I starting asking around — 'who here has ever written a hit?' And somebody said Maurice Williams."

Born and raised in South Carolina, Maurice Williams grew up in the church, and had channeled his love of music, and natural talent for theatricality and showmanship, into a decent career on the nightclub circuit. He was the songwriter, frontman and lead singer for the Glad-

Maurice Williams, left, and the Zodiacs, circa 1960. The national No. 1 "Stay" was the first song produced under Johnny McCullough and Phil Gernhard's Briarwood Enterprises banner in Columbia — and Briarwood's only hit. Herald Records publicity photo.

iolas, a sextet that blended doo-wop, rhythm 'n' blues balladry and the smooth pop harmonies made popular by other black vocal groups like the Platters, the Flamingos and the Drifters.

Like many regional performers, they cut single records one at a time, on a series of tiny labels, as financing materialized. This was the Jim Crow South, and golden opportunities did not often present themselves, particularly for black musicians.

In 1957 the Diamonds — a white Canadian vocal group - had taken Williams' quirky doo-wop song "Little Darlin'" to No. 4 on the national chart, while the Gladiolas' original had barely scraped the Top 40. Although "whitening" R&B records for radio play was common (if unfortunate) practice at the time, Williams was not exactly thrilled that his best song — at least he thought so - had been co-opted into a big hit for *anybody* else.

After a summer '59 show in Columbia, Williams and his group, now called the Zodiacs, met USC roommates Vince Cole and Phil Gernhard.

They introduced themselves as musicians — Cole played guitar, and Gernhard was a drummer — and as it turned out they were huge fans of R&B and doo-wop. The original records, which they heard at night via Nashville AM radio, and not the watered-down, whitened-up versions by the likes of Pat Boone or the Diamonds.

And they had a little money. And they were interested in using it to cut some sides for their "company," Cole Records.

Just what Maurice Williams wanted to hear.

Recorded, like most tiny-budget records of the period, in tinny and single-take monophonic, neither "Golly Gee" nor its followup "Lover (Where Are You)" made a ripple outside of the dance halls in Columbia. Both were slow, romantic ballads.

Still, it's not hard to imagine the young pals and their girlfriends, up late with the HiFi and fueled by tequila, dancing and shaking to the Zodiacs' exotic, erotic B-side "T Town" (that's T for *Tijuana*) with its throbbing tenor sax solo, a record they'd made themselves. Getting excited about going to an early class the next morning? Probably not.

Stan Hardin, a local guitarist, introduced Johnny McCullough to Phil Gernhard, the go-getting, red-headed college kid with a passion for R&B. Over a couple of beers, McCullough explained that he was starting a Columbia-based production company.

"He found out I was a producer and he wanted to know if he could help, and be a part," McCullough remembered. "He wanted to be in the music business. I knew he'd be a good promoter.

"I realized there was something there that I could pick up on. I knew he had some talent. I knew he could make it in the music industry."

Gernhard had the added advantage of knowing Maurice Williams personally.

They named their company Briarwood Enterprises, after the street where the McCulloughs lived, Briarwood Road. The company consisted of McCullough and Gernhard, McCullough's brother Jimmy, and the siblings' dad, J.C. McCullough, who handled the books.

They started writing songs together, and called their publishing division "Windsong Music."

Phil took a job at the Star-Lite Drive-In theater, and booked a few concerts featuring local bands. McCullough and Hardin started a dance band they called the Archers.

And they all waited for Maurice Williams and the Zodiacs to come back to Columbia.

The only thing that could even pass for a recording studio in Columbia was a ribbed steel Quonset hut out on Shakespeare Road, on property owned by WCOS, the local AM station. From 1953 to '56, it was also the home of WCOS-TV, the very first television outlet in the entire state of South Carolina. An ABC affiliate, WCOS proudly beamed *The Adventures of Ozzie & Harriet, The Lone Ranger* and other prime-time favorites from the nation's "third" network to rabbit-ear black and white TVs all over Columbia and the surrounding rural areas.

Engineer Homer Fesperman wasn't idle during the station's six-year hiatus (it would roar back with a vengeance in '61, then live long and prosper in the community). The place had a mono, single-track recording deck, so it was leased out for radio commercials, advertising jingles and — if anyone were so inclined — cutting records.

Gernhard, of course, knew the "studio" from his Cole Records experience.

Since then, however, Williams and his group had traveled all over the southeast, and made another single ("College Girl") on another shoestring local label (Selwyn Records, in Charlotte).

Sometime late in the summer of 1960, Maurice Williams and the Zodiacs filed into the WCOS Quonset hut and cut a demo of "Stay," an innocuously catchy song Williams had written back in '53 — when he was barely 15 - but never got around to recording. It was Johnny McCullough's first time in a real studio. At 19, Phil Gernhard was a veteran.

The instruments had to be balanced live in the room; there was no "mixing" to speak of. Nor was there the opportunity for overdubbing or "dropping in" edits to fix the occasional bum note or botched lyric. "One mistake, and we went back to the top," McCullough said of the session. Stan Hardin played additional guitar.

At day's end, all involved knew the WCOS demo of "Stay" was something special. It was impossible to get the song out of your head. And it practically begged you to dance.

McCullough took his bravado, and the tapes of Briarwood's very first session, straight to New York to shop for a record deal. "I went to 13 labels," he said. "They all turned me down. But I *knew* I had a hit!

"I went in to see Al Silver at Herald Records, and the secretary said 'You can't see him.' So I sat down outside the door, and she said 'What are you doing?' I said 'I'm going to sit outside the door here, because eventually he's gonna have to leave — and I'll see him if I have to sit here all night long.' She finally brought me in.

"We played the tape, and he said 'You got a hit record. I want to put it out,' and I said 'We can do it better.' He said 'Leave it alone.'"

Gernhard always told a slightly different version of this somewhat apocryphal tale: He'd been there in Al Silver's office, too. "The song wasn't recorded at a high enough level," he said. "None of us knew what the hell we were doing. Silver drew a VU meter for us, and said, 'Go back and re-record it, and keep the needle up in this area.' We took the piece of paper with us.

"Also, it had a line in it that they found objectionable: 'Let's have another smoke.' He said radio wouldn't play anything that encouraged young people to smoke."

Suitably chastised, the novice producers returned to Columbia, called in Williams and his group, and cut a second version — keeping Silver's drawing on the console where they could see it. With the requested edits, "Stay" clocked in at 1:39, short even for the standards of the era.

Gernhard loved to relate how Silver had instructed them to record it "flat," meaning without the use of echo or embellishment on the lead vocal, but they thought Silver was instructing Williams to sing it slightly off-key. This was seriously discussed at the session, but they agreed it didn't make any sense.

Recalled Williams: "When he said to sing it flat, it hurt us, because from the time we were in glee club, all we knew was to sing on key. But Silver said 'If you want a contact, you have to sing it flat so the average man in the street can sing it.' I said 'OK, we'll do it,' and I came up with 'Stay — aahhhh - just a little bit longer,' and sang the first part flat."

Zodiac Henry "Shane" Gaston provided the sky-high falsetto vocal that made "Stay" so indelible.

In time, McCullough related, "I went back up there, and Silver started playin' the new tape. He just looked at me. He didn't move a muscle, didn't change his expression or anything.

"When it got through, he looked at me and said 'You know what you did, John?' I said 'What's that?'

"He said 'You took a hit record that you thought wasn't good enough, you had to go and change it ... you took a hit record and you turned it into a f–kin' smash!'

"And that was the first time he changed his expression. He smiled. And I thought I had screwed up."

"Stay," produced by "Briarwood Enterprises," was released in October, and in a few weeks — Nov. 21, 1960 to be precise - it reached the top of the national pop charts. Johnny and Phil were No. 1 with their first collaboration.

(Thirty years later, after its inclusion on the multi-platinum *Dirty Dancing* soundtrack album, the Record Industry Association of America announced that the Maurice Williams and the Zodiacs' recording of "Stay" had sold some eight million copies.)

Not long after "Stay" became a smash, and the Briarwood brain trust

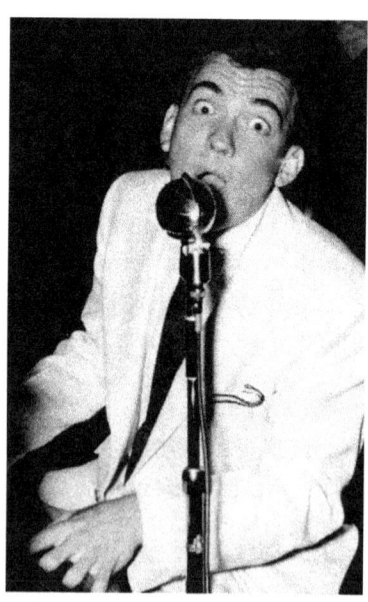

When Louisiana piano-playing hepcat Dick Holler arrived in Columbia, Gernhard's world changed. Family photo.

had finished up with buying rounds and congratulating each other on their infallible ears and business acumen, the search began for the next big record. Al Silver paid McCullough and Gernhard to produce an entire *Stay* album for Maurice Williams and the Zodiacs, and 10 out of the 14 tracks included were published by Windsong, but Gernhard was already restless. He wanted a new challenge.

It came in the form of Don Smith, the garrulous bass player for a Louisiana R&B quartet called Dick Holler and the Rockets. Smith was hitch-hiking back to Baton Rouge; Gernhard picked him along a South Carolina highway.

When the ensuing conversation revealed that Smith was a musician, Gernhard naturally asked him if he had written any songs. Smith replied yes, he was a writer, but the guy Gernhard really needed to connect with was Dick Holler himself, a singer and boogie-woogie piano player, a soulful man and a songwriter with a steamer trunk full of cool tunes.

In the late '50s, Holler — who played rollicking barroom piano Professor Longhair-style and sang in a swampy, hep-cat swagger of a voice like a white Fats Domino - cut a handful of unsuccessful sides for a tiny Louisiana label. Like most regional musicians, he and the band were eking out a living playing nightclubs and hiring out, and crossing their fingers that something would click.

Every one of Briarwood's post-"Stay" singles by Maurice Williams flopped — there was no momentum to speak of, and Gernhard and McCullough had to sell their share of the song's publishing to keep the lights on. McCullough played Archers gigs, and Gernhard produced and promoted local dance shows.

But they never stopped looking for their Next Big Thing.

Gernhard heard something he loved in Dick Holler's stax-o-wax, and summoned the group to Columbia to cut a couple of sides in the Quonset hut studio. The band's name was changed to the more commercial Dick Holler and the Holidays.

Holler and his three bandmates rented a house together and settled in. A deal was forged with Comet Records, a subsidiary of Al Silver's Herald. Their first single, "King Kong," was part R&B — in fact, the four white guys sounded they might have been the Zodiacs under another name - and part novelty record (with "jungle" sound effects provided by McCullough and Gernhard).

Now, who is the toughest cat we know? (King Kong from the Amazon!)
He's sixty feet tall from head to toe (King Kong from the Amazon!)

The followup, "Mooba Grooba," was pure New Orleans rock 'n' roll fun, catchy and silly with nonsense lyrics, and unabashedly dance-ready.

Great googa mooga shooga, thought I saw a mooba grooba walkin' down the railroad track
It ain't been gone for very very long and I hope it won't come back!

They both should've been big hits with the jive-crazy Columbia kids. But they weren't, and neither was Holler's third collaboration with Gernhard and McCullough. Written by Smith and another Louisiana rocker, Cyril Vetter, "Double Shot (of My Baby's Love)" was a party singalong, with a Mardi Gras, carnival atmosphere and vaguely sexual lyrics.

Columbia radio loved the Holidays' single, but the nation at large never caught on. "Double Shot" would become a Top 20 hit in 1966 with a watered-down version by the Swingin' Medallions, another South Carolina group.

Holler, right, and the Holidays, broke down again on a highway outside Columbia, circa 1962. Family photo.

The Holidays sometimes played backup on other artists' Briarwood recordings, although they had quickly become an extremely popular live act in Columbia and were drawing steady paychecks. In the Carolinas, the dance-pop hits of the day were known as "beach music."

Holler, being from Louisiana, wasn't altogether sure what "beach music" was, but he was more than happy to appease the locals because they kept the money flowing. He loved Columbia.

Between 1961 and '63, Johnny and Phil took running jumps at the brass ring again and again, one record at a time. The prevailing logic was to throw everything against the wall and see what stuck. With luck, they'd get another "Stay" out of somebody.

They produced doo-wop and pop vocal singles by the Monograms, Dale & the Del Hearts, a pair of Duane Eddy-like instrumentals by guitarist Clark Summit and a teen-dream pop confection by Elvis soundalike Jimmy Rand.

("Clark Summit" was the stage name of Dennis Coffey, who would go on to become a studio player for Motown Records — an integral part of the legendary Funk Brothers band.)

They were constantly on the lookout for ways to snag a few extra bucks by sharing (or co-opting) their artists' publishing. The B-side of the Holidays' "Mooba Grooba" was the McCullough-penned "Hey Little Fool." Both sides of Jimmy Rand's single were written by McCullough, McCullough and Gernhard, and — of course - published by Windsong.

They "discovered" the Columbia-area singing group called the Anglos, with singers Thelma Bynum (who used the stage name Linda Martell) and her sister Julie Gibson, their musician brother Lee Martell and a cousin named Barbara.

According to Linda Martell's granddaughter Quia Thompson, Lee "wrote all their songs, and played the keys. The other band members changed out, here and there."

The Anglos, she said, started at school talent shows "and never lost."

In 1962 Briarwood produced Herald 575, "I Got News For You" (by "Julie Gibson and the Anglows") backed with "You've Been Cheatin' On Me" (by "The Angloes Featuring Barbara"). McCullough was credited as composer of both songs, with the A-side naming "The Holidays/Stan Hardin guitar" as the musicians. Holler's New Orleans piano playing is unmistakable. The carefully-arranged lead and background vocals are very like the Shirelles or the Cookies, girl groups from the era.

Side B is a different story. "You've Been Cheatin' on Me" is much more low-fi that the perky A-side. It's a raw recording — it sounds like a demo — with just guitar and drums backing up Cousin Barbara's gutsy vocal. There's nothing else there, no "arrangement," and it's very effective.

Next came Fire 512, "A Little Tear (Was Falling From My Eyes)" by "Linda Martell and the Anglos." Very similar in song structure to "I Got News For You," it, too, credited McCullough as composer. On the B-side, "The Things I Do For You," the songwriters were listed as James McCullough/P. Gernhard.

In the late 1960s, Linda Martell would become the first female African American county singer; she sang at the Grand Ole Opry and appeared on "Hee Haw." Monument Records publicity photo.

Martell's granddaughter believes Lee Martell actually composed all four Anglos songs.

"There is a chance," Quia Thompson said, "my uncle 'sold his publishing' or maybe he was tricked out of it, I don't know. But I do know that those songs, all the songs they recorded, are his. He was a brilliant musician and was respected as such."

"A Little Tear" would, years later, become one of the most revered and sought-after early '60s "girl group" records to be created in the Carolinas. Even though it didn't sell in '62.

Linda Martell went on to make history, in 1969, as the first Black woman to record a country music album, and to appear on TV's *Hee-Haw*. Beyonce gave Martell several shout-outs, as a pioneering artist, on her 2024 album *Cowboy Carter*.

In the middle of all the Briarwood excitement, Gernhard — now a budding mogul - simply stopped going to class. He'd lost interest in anything but music and the bohemian lifestyle he was living with his friends.

He brought a pretty, dark-haired girl home to Sarasota and introduced her as his wife. Boyd, Sara and Judee — home on break from Florida State University — greeted her warmly, but with genuine surprise. He'd never mentioned her before.

Since no record of a legal union exists in any available database, it's possible that Phil just lied to his family so they'd allow his girlfriend into the house. Although his parents assured him they were proud of what he'd done with "Stay," Phil was in hot water for abandoning college — and the military — to pursue record-making.

But that wasn't going well, either. "We were trying to make hit records," said McCullough. "We tried to write songs together ... we did a lot of stuff, but the only ones that we really hit on were Maurice's."

In early 1963, Briarwood breathed its last with the one and only record by the Archers, the Columbia show band featuring Stan Hardin and Johnny McCullough. Written by all three band members, "Hey Rube" was performed in the goofy, call-and-response style of the Coasters.

On the other side, "Unwind It" (credited to McCullough-Gernhard) was a 180 degree turn, a frat-house singalong, Wonder-bread white and undistinguished. The two songs might as well have been recorded by two different groups.

Briarwood was able to get "Hey Rube" released on Laurie Records, a New York-based national label which had made its name through teen dream and doo-wop hits by the likes of Dion & the Belmonts and the Mystics.

Like everything else since "Stay," however, the Archers' single was destined for the compost heap. Briarwood Enterprises breathed no more.

Gernhard had no choice but to go home to Florida, placate his father and re-enroll in school. He chose pre-law, which he figured would make Boyd happy.

Said sister Judee: "He'd gotten off track. When you're 18, 19 years old, everything is visceral. He was living a double life — it wouldn't have been anything they'd have chosen for him. Dad and Mom didn't know anything about the business.

"The Coles and the McCulloughs weren't businessmen — it was very much artist-by-artist and song-by-song. He made a ton of money, and he lost a ton of money trying to make some more money with what he had."

When Phil arrived home, tail between his legs, Boyd Gernhard was just finishing up a three-year term as a Sarasota County Commissioner, a proud and loud achievement he never let anyone forget. Boyd magnanimously "allowed" his son to re-enter the family, despite his failure in South Carolina.

4

I Want More

"I decided to go to Tampa for the old three-year law program and then transfer to Stetson. It was going to be tough, but I figured I'd make my dad happy. He wasn't too turned-on about music for me."
Phil Gernhard

Almost as soon as he started attending pre-law classes at the University of Tampa, Gernhard was introduced to a pretty, doe-eyed blonde from St. Petersburg named Sandy Thompson. She was dating his roommate, and they were introduced at a party on campus.

"As soon as my eyes locked onto his, I thought 'This is it for me. I'm done.'"

The romance began inauspiciously. "He asked my work cohort out for lunch, and that almost crushed me," Sandy said. "He just did things like that to see if he could get your attention." Phil, she came to find out, loved drama.

Soon enough, they began dating. Thompson, who'd grown up in a rigidly Catholic home, admired Gernhard's quiet determination. "He never verbalized it," she said. "He was one of those guys that just did it." He was, she discovered, a thinker, a reader, a man with an almost insatiable curiosity about anything and everything. He always seemed to have a plan.

Phil regaled her with stories of the recording studio, where he felt like an artist face to face with a blank canvas; he created with sound. It was

Phil and Sandy, on the lookout for a new group at the Sarasota Surfers Club, circa 1965. The weekend-only, non-alcoholic dance club was limited to teenagers; if you were 20, you couldn't get in. Family photo.

in the studio, he told her, that he put both the analytical and the creative sides of his brain together. There was no other feeling that came close.

And he romanced her, hard.

From a letter to Sandy, dated March 2, 1964:

It's been a long time since I have believed in the really good things in life. All I have known is continued disillusionment and a whole lot of filth. The way I have lived for the last 4 years, I am deeply ashamed of. Ashamed because I know how one should live but I regretted it. Of course, I had good reasons I thought, but knowing you has made me wonder.

Yours,

Phil

From a letter to Sandy's Uncle Buddy, who was at the time studying for the priesthood:

She showed me a life that I had previously scoffed at. Life for me was a self-ish world of pleasure, deceit, dishonor and sin. But this is what I had known, and I believed that the other type was fiction...

...But as time passed and she held firm, even though she loved me, I began to want to share her world with her. If this included her church, fine, for I had no God, let alone a church...

...We are now, as you know, in the process of trying to get my previous marriage invalidated, for we can be married in the church. To both of us this will in fact be my first and only marriage. I do not feel that what happened in the past was in God's eyes a marriage, because there was no union of spirit or person or anything ... I feel in my heart God knew that there was no marriage. I do not blame the church for not sharing my view because they don't know or can know what really took place.

Despite what Sandy believed were Phil's best efforts, he was never able to have that "first marriage" annulled, and the subject was dropped.

Eventually, Phil told Sandy about his love/hate relationship with his father. "Mom Gernhard was the one who really controlled the ship," Sandy recalled. "Phil said 'Mom passed Dad the ball, and he fumbled.' And that stuck with me forever."

She found Boyd Gernhard intimidating. "He was really, really stern, a tough taskman. Phil never got as tall as his dad or any of those psycho-logical principles. He was always a little bit shorter than him."

Not only that, "He was a staunch Republican, and he was a bigot. He didn't like Jewish people, he didn't like Black people, and he wasn't afraid to talk about it. He said the thing he liked best about me was my nose, because it was little."

Nevertheless, Bud and his son had raised the white flag when Phil returned to Florida from South Carolina. They both wanted it to work, but they were both stubborn and didn't like to admit it when they were wrong.

"I entered Tampa with the same arch-conservative ideas that had been passed through my family for generations, you know, 'love moth-erhood, hate blacks, make money, that kind of stuff," Gernhard would tell the UT alumni magazine.

Eventually, his thinking changed, thanks to the ongoing political and social discourse at college ("in the midst of the rah rah Goldwater generation, under a professor with extreme rightist opinions," he said).

Phil realized that "with such divergent views, obviously both can't be right. But does that mean that either is totally wrong? Suddenly my black and white world started taking on new shading and color I had never noticed before."

He made the Honor Roll at UT, and then the Dean's List, and he aced an early acceptance exam into Stetson University College of Law in St. Petersburg.

Gernhard told his girlfriend about his fantasy of becoming a great trial lawyer. "He wanted to be Clarence Darrow," she recalled. "Dramatic, the kind you write movies about. That was his thing. He would've never made it as a corporate lawyer."

And he began to frequent the St. Petersburg and Tampa-area nightclubs where live music was featured. Sure, he was on the straight-arrow track and bound for a law degree and the respectable career his parents wanted for him, but the allure of rock 'n' roll, and of getting to be a part of it, was just too much.

"I went everywhere Phil went," Sandy said. "Music, music, music."

In July 1964, Dick and Marge Sexton opened St. Petersburg's first teen nightclub. The Sextons already managed the outdoor Silver Star Skating Rink, which had live bands on the weekends — but as Marge Sexton told the *Evening Independent* soon after the new club opened its doors, they'd discovered a void.

"Many high school students come here," she explained, "but 19-year-olds are the predominant age group. There seems to be a vacuum for them: too old for high school dances, and too young for adult night clubs. We're trying to fill a community need."

Located in a tiny strip of stores right on Madeira Beach, the Surfer's Club became THE place to go in St. Pete. Most of the beach was yet to be developed — the towering, view-blocking condominiums that would come to dominate the area were many years away — and so the kids built bonfires, played music and danced on the beach behind the club into the wee hours (or until curfew).

With a capacity of 400, and a strict no-alcohol policy, the Surfer's Club was open six nights a week. Kids paid $1 for a yearly "membership" — they were given a card, personally signed by one of the supervising Sextons — and charged a 75-cent admission on live band nights. Non-members got in for a dollar.

Chaperones lurked discreetly in the shadows, ostensibly to discourage dirty dancing, but trouble rarely reared its head. "Here they let us act like teen-agers," said a young man to the *Independent*. "It's not like other dances, where adults patrol the dancing."

In the wake of the Beatles' arrival, and the musical tsunami that followed, garage bands were popping up in every city and town in America. St. Petersburg, Tampa and the surrounding municipalities were no exception. Bands with names like the Intruders, the Outsiders, the Enticers, the Tempests, the Surprize and the Rovin' Flames made the rounds of dances and sock-hops, and as 1964 turned into '65, the Surfer's Club was competing head-to-boot with the Spot, Tampa's happening hangout for teens.

With members from both sides of Tampa Bay, the Tropics were an energetic, horn-based "show band" with stage uniforms, dance steps and a talented lead singer named Mel Dwyer.

At their Surfer's Club audition, the Sextons liked the Tropics so much they offered them a management contract and the gig as house band - with the proviso that they (a) get rid of the horns and (b) become more of a "Beatle-type" band.

The Tropics agreed.

Gernhard, meanwhile, was 24 years old and hungry. He wanted to re-experience that euphoric feeling he'd had when "Stay" hit No. 1. Law school was still his priority, he assured Sandy, but the Next Big Thing was out there somewhere, he was sure of it. All he had to do was find it and work that Gernhard magic.

He was a frequent visitor to the Surfer's Club. "Phil was a record producer, but he was out of work," Marge Sexton recalled, "and he needed to find something to do. We had decided to expand Surfer's Club, so we asked Phil if that might be something you'd be interested in? And he was very interested in that. So we opened a Surfer's Club in Sarasota."

The Sarasota teen club was only open on weekends. Phil and Sandy would drive down on Friday afternoons, after his last class of the day and after she clocked out at First National Bank, and open the place up. To save money, they stayed with Mom and Dad Gernhard at the family home on Bayshore Road, across the street from Sarasota Jungle Gardens.

It was, Sandy remembered, an amendment to the "temporary peace" between father and son. "He stayed in his room and I stayed in mine," she explained. "He used to slide me these little love notes under the door."

Whenever some national act with a fresh hit came through, the Sextons would double-book them, for one night at the St. Pete club, the next night in Sarasota. It was cheaper that way.

"He wasn't really that ambitious," Sexton recalled, "but he was pretty good. I liked him, but he really didn't do a super job running the Surfer's Club. It wasn't what we expected out of him. He had high hopes that he would make a big success of it."

The Sarasota club closed, inauspiciously. But Gernhard had his foot in the door. He was dying to get into a recording studio.

His first local production was a Tampa pop quartet called the Sugar Beats, one of his favorites from the local club circuit. "Phil was hustling and trying to get it done," remembered Kent LaVoie, the band's rhythm guitarist and singer. "We were there in the right place at the right time; that's all that amounted to."

He took the band into H&H Productions, a tiny, two-track studio in Tampa used primarily for radio jingles and commercials, operated by disc jockey Chuck Harder and his business partner, Phil Kempen. (Harder would go on to fame as the creator of The Peoples Radio Network, and longtime host of the widely syndicated political talk show *For the People*).

For the A-side, the potential hit, Gernhard chose "What Am I Doing Here With You," a song he'd heard on Johnny Rivers' first album, *In Action*. "The way it worked out," LaVoie said, "was I was the only one who sounded good singing on tape, so I just overdubbed all the harmony parts. It's over-fast and it's hokey, but it was 'original,' from the Tampa/St. Pete area."

Gernhard cut a deal with Knight Records to press the single; he ordered 500 copies, and hand-delivered it to all the local Top 40 stations. Others he mailed out, although "What Am I Doing Here" (as it was called on the label) did not cause a stir of any sort outside Florida.

Tampa's Sugar Beats, with future star Kent LaVoie, second from left, on guitar and vocals, at the Surfers Club, 1965. The first band Phil recorded after his return to Florida. Family photo.

From a letter to Sandy, dated Aug. 25, 1965:

The Beats record is selling better. Ron's Record Shop has sold out & wants another 30 more. Great huh. Wish it would move in St. Pete as well.

Love always,

Phil

For LaVoie, a native of Winter Haven who'd flunked out of both the University of South Florida and St. Petersburg Junior College, having a hit — even something so relatively insignificant as a regional hit — was enough to make him tune out just about everything else. The Sugar Beats went from making $60 a show to $300, simply because they had a record. "Everybody did it, but no record was played as much as ours," LaVoie recalled. "You couldn't get away from it."

With "What Am I Doing Here," Gernhard had made his first pure rock 'n' roll record, and was undeterred by the Sugar Beats' relative failure. He was intoxicated by the experience, and he enjoyed his newfound notoriety. At the urging of Marge Sexton, he approached the Tropics, then the biggest band in the area.

"Phil was an energetic, creative guy with lots of great ideas and of course, he had a way in to record companies," said the band's bassist Charlie Souza. "So we were stoked."

Gernhard drove out to the Surfer's Club on a weekend afternoon, where the Tropics were rehearsing. During a smoke break in the parking lot, he suggested they come up with an all-new song to record, with him, at H&H.

"As the sugar sand was blowing in the breeze, Phil came up with the idea of the song 'I Want More,'" said Souza. "He practically wrote it for us on the hood of his car as the five band members threw in an occasional line, and came up with some licks and chord changes, and a melody line to match the lyric ideas. After a quick hour or two, we had it worked up in the club and were ready to record."

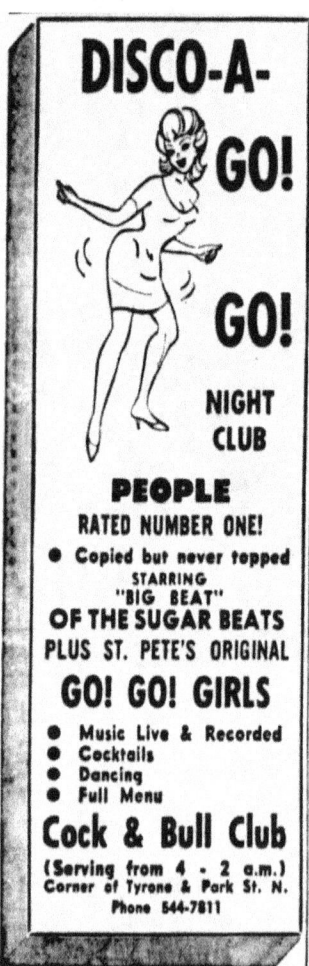
Gernhard produced the Tropics' version of "I Want More" at H&H. Again, it went out via Knight Records. The band's dominance of their home turf continued, as the single was all the rage on local AM stations WLCY and WALT.

The Tropics' single — a guitar-riff raver rich with echo and energy -

sold in great numbers to their loyal Tampa Bay area fans, and always drew the kids onto the floor at dance shows. But that was about it.

The Outsiders, including teenage Ronny Elliott (top right) who would soon play a major role in Gernhard's business dealings. Courtesy of Ronny Elliott.

Gernhard then turned his attention to another band of hopeful young scruffs, the Outsiders. It was Surfer's Club matriarch Marge Sexton who made the introductions, recalled band member Ronny Elliott. "She said 'We've got this great new connection. He's going to come and start doing stuff with us. He's got all these connections and he's going to want to record you.'"

The teenaged Outsiders looked up to their new Svengali. "He was basically a kid," Elliott said, "but to us, he was an old businessman."

The band had a swampy, back-alley sound, with sharp, stinging guitars playing boogie and blues riffs, and a singer who sneered and drawled (the Rolling Stones were at the peak of their Top 40 popularity at the time).

In the first months of 1966, the Outsiders cut two Gernhard-produced singles on Knight: "Just Let Me Be" and a remake of Eddie Cochran's "Summertime Blues," which had become a mid '60s teen-party anthem.

The records, as per the pattern, didn't do anything outside of Tampa Bay, nor did a second Tropics single, a raver called "You Better Move," with vocalist Mel Dryer in full screaming-bloody-hell Mick Jagger mode.

"You Better Move" was significant for Gernhard, however. Because of his previous dealings with them, he was able to convince brothers Gene and Bob Schwartz of New York-based Laurie Records to release the single nationally.

And with "You Better Move," Gernhard had moved up in the world, leaving the cramped, two-track mono studios of H&H behind. The track was recorded at a brand-new facility on MacDill Avenue, in South Tampa, Charles Fuller Productions.

Charles Fuller Hunt was a sound engineer who'd produced a few bands, at H&H, for his own label, Boss. Charles Fuller Productions, a four-track recording studio (state of the art for the mid 1960s) opened for business the summer of 1966.

Most of Fuller's work came from the world of advertising — radio jingles, commercials, marching band recordings and soundtracks for school productions.

Once word got out that Fuller had four tracks — and a nice-sized studio floor — nobody booked H&H any more.

By the time the Outsiders cut their third single, there'd been an upset. A band from Cleveland — also called the Outsiders — had released a single called "Time Won't Let Me," on giant Capitol Records.

Gernhard had told the Tampa Outsiders, when "Time Won't Let Me" had first appeared, that it would never be a hit, and they wouldn't have to change their name because the Ohio group would sink and be forgotten.

But his golden ear let him down, and "Time Won't Let Me" by the Outsiders from Ohio was a smash, spending 10 weeks on the chart and peaking at No. 5.

And so the Outsiders — the band from Tampa — became the Soul

Trippers.

For the band's debut single on Providence, Laurie's R&B subsidiary, they chose a blues standard — the sexually charged "I'm a King Bee," by Louisiana singer, songwriter and blues harmonica player James "Slim Harpo" Moore. The Rolling Stones included a version on their first album.

Ronny Elliott: "When we went in to record 'King Bee,' the Laurie people said 'Well, you know, it's a little explicit for radio. Let's see if we can get some more vanilla lyrics.' So Phil wrote a letter to Slim Harpo saying 'Is there any chance you could give us some lyrics that might get on radio?'

"It was too late, anyway. We'd come up with our own watered-down version and recorded it — and this letter comes to Phil. It's three or four pages, all hand-written, from Slim Harpo. All new lyrics to 'King Bee' — the vilest, filthiest, most disgusting things.

"Now, how much would I give to have that letter! If for nothing else just to sell it on eBay. But Phil didn't keep it. He just didn't have any interest in that kind of thing. He didn't have a sentimental bone in his body."

Gernhard was having so much fun "discovering" and recording Tampa Bay bands, law school — and pleasing his father — went on the back burner. "His mother said 'He's chasing that pie in the sky,'" Sandy Gernhard remembered. "And she'd plead, Sandy, it's up to you — you've got to make him stop.' And I'm thinking 'Yeah, Mom, I'm working on it.'"

She had no intention of "stopping" Phil, because she knew he couldn't be swayed. Still, "He wanted it to work so badly here. He wanted the family thing to work that much. We'd go down there for Christmas, and they'd come up to our house for Thanksgiving. Phil wanted that tight-knit family situation."

Gernhard discussed this period of waffling in his interview with the University of Tampa alumni magazine. "Law school," he said, "was a big disappointment. I had expected it to take off from the great experience I'd had at UT, but it was a bore, memorizing law after law.

"Some of the older guys said stick around, it gets better in the more advanced courses. But by the end of the first year my average had dropped to a C, and I had lost my scholarship. So I was operating a teenage nightclub in Sarasota and booking dance bands to pay my tuition."

5

In the Nick of Time, a Hero Arose

THE ROYAL GUARDSMEN — SNOOPY VS. THE RED BARON. Tongue-in-cheek rocker based on "Snoopy" of "Peanuts" fame could prove a giant novelty seller. Well produced and performed featuring a solid rhythm dance beat. (Laurie 3366).

> Billboard
> "Top 60 Spotlight"
> Dec. 10, 1966

In October of 1965, cartoonist Charles M. Schulz introduced a new storyline to his popular comic strip *Peanuts*, which appeared in pretty much every newspaper in the country, seven days a week. Snoopy, the wisecracking, anthropomorphic black and white dog whose imaginary exploits had turned him into the strip's breakout star, began to fancy himself the pilot of a World War I biplane, doing battle with a German foe, the Red Baron.

Snoopy sat atop his white clapboard doghouse, which he referred to as a Sopwith Camel ("Can you think of a funnier name for an airplane?" Schulz said), his forearms stretched out straight in front like mounted machine guns.

The Royal Guardsmen, taken at Ocala's Six Gun territory in the fall of 1966. Clockwise from left: Chris Nunley, Billy Taylor, Bill Balogh, Tom Richards, John Burdett and Barry Winslow. Taylor, Burdett and Winslow are wearing wigs, because they were still in high school, where long hair was strictly forbidden. Laurie Records publicity photo.

There had been actual Sopwith Camels, and a real Red Baron, in the first world war. Manfred von Richthofen was a *Luftstreitkrafte* fighter pilot with an impressive record of 80 Allied "kills." Flying a bright red Fokker triplane, von Richthofen was the scourge of the skies, a flying devil awarded the Blue Max — Germany's highest military honor — by Kaiser Wilhelm himself.

None of this meant much to Americans in the mid 1960s, until Schulz, inspired by a model Fokker in his young son's room, made the (never-seen) Baron his comic strip beagle's arch-enemy. Sporting goggles and a jaunty scarf, Snoopy - through thought balloons - created an adventurous fantasy storyline for himself: *Here's the World War I flying ace walking out onto the field* ...

Snoopy engaged the Red Baron in tense plane-to-plane combat ... and always lost, crashing to the ground (in his mind) atop the smoking carcass of his Sopwith Camel. Then he'd plot revenge.

Readers couldn't get enough of Snoopy's exploits, and by the spring of '66, Schulz was in overdrive, cranking out new Red Baron storylines one after another.

Schulz published a cash-in picture book for children, *Snoopy and the*

Peanuts creator Charles M. Schulz turned Snoopy and the Red Baron *into a top-selling book in 1966. Fawcett Crest Books.*

Red Baron, with the thrill-seeking canine on a multi-page adventure. The book was an enormous hit, and America found itself more or less in the grip of Beaglemania. Everyone loved Snoopy and his ridiculous flights of fancy.

"*Peanuts* was one of Mom and Dad Gernhard's favorite comics," Sandy said. "We used to all discuss the cartoon when we went down there."

This made Gernhard, sitting in one boring law seminar after another, flash back to a Dick Holler session he'd produced in '62, at Cosimo Matassa's J&M Studio in New Orleans.

Holler had been a huge fan of singer/songwriter Johnny Horton's hit recordings of the story-songs "The Battle of New Orleans" and "Sink the Bismarck," which set the facts of real historical events to sing-along choruses, sly humor and march-time military drumming. Horton's "The Battle of New Orleans" won the 1960 Grammy as the year's best country and western record.

"I had always been something of an aviation freak," Holler reflected. "I thought 'Wow, if there are gonna be pop records here that are historical, I'll write a song about my favorite pilot, the Red Baron.'"

The song began with Holler speaking over guitar and a steady military drumbeat: "You know, back in 1916 during World War I, a lot of new inventions made their way to the front lines: The tank, the machine gun, poison gas. But the greatest innovation of all was the fighter plane. This, then is the story of the greatest fighter pilot who took to the skies during World War I: He was Germany's Manfred von Richthofen, the Red Baron!"

As his boogie-woogie piano joined the fray, Holler began to sing:

After the turn of the century
In the clear blue skies over Germany
Came a roar and a thunder men had never heard
Like the screamin' sound of a big warbird.
Baron von Richthofen was his name
He ruled the skies in his blood-red plane
Eighty men tried, and eighty men died
Now they're buried together on the countryside.
Ten, twenty, thirty, forty, fifty or more!
The bloody Red Baron was rolling up a score!
Eighty men died trying to end the spree

Of the bloody Red Baron of Germany!

Holler and his band spent an entire day at J&M recording "The Red Baron," with Gernhard helping out behind the board.

"We had the whole thing cut — the verses, the melody, the chorus, the machine guns, the airplane sounds, all that stuff was totally finished," Holler said. "It was just like those Johnny Horton records, except we put in really serious machine gun and airplane sounds. And taking off and landing sounds. Cosmo did it all on spec; he wouldn't have got involved if he didn't think it was a possibility."

But Horton the historical hero was gone, killed in an auto accident, and the public's enthusiasm for his quirky, Southern brand of high-stepping patriotic singalongs apparently died along with him. "Cosmo had a lot of muscle," said Holler. "He took it to all his friends, man, and he couldn't get anybody to put it out." Therefore, Dick Holler and the Holidays' "The Red Baron" never saw the light of day.

Phil and Sandy were married in Sarasota on Aug. 6, 1966, with Carl Troxell, a local DJ whose air name was Charlie Brown, serving as Best Man. The bride was given away by Boyd Gernhard. After a honeymoon trip to New Orleans, they settled into a modest home in St. Petersburg, close to Stetson College of Law and not far from Sandy's widowed mom.

Gernhard had abandoned Johnny McCullough, Briarwood Enterprises, Maurice Williams and South Carolina. He was, or so his father wanted desperately to believe, a happily married, upwardly mobile law student.

Except he hated it.

One July morning, Gernhard began making notes on his yellow legal pad. Wouldn't it be great if Snoopy — the most beloved cartoon character on the planet — could be worked into Dick Holler's old storyline? Wouldn't that be funny?

Holler's song only had two verses, followed by the "Ten, twenty, thirty ..." chorus. In a Stetson University lecture hall, Gernhard started to create additional lyrics to the existing melody:

In the nick of time, a hero arose
A funny-looking dog with a big black nose
He flew into the sky to seek revenge
But the baron shot him down — curses, foiled again!

Then back to
Ten, twenty, thirty, forty, fifty or more!
The bloody Red Baron was rollin' up the score!
Eighty men died trying to end that spree
Of the bloody Red Baron of Germany!

"I took the basic Red Baron idea — or as much of it as I could recall — and wrote in Snoopy because I dug the strip, and I really dug the dog," Gernhard would say. "Then I sang it to my wife. She looked at me like I was crazy."

Positive reinforcement.

Now Snoopy had sworn that he'd get than man
So he asked the Great Pumpkin for a new battle plan
He challenged the German to a real dogfight
While the baron was laughing, he got him in his sights
That bloody Red Baron was in a fix
He tried everything, but he'd run out of tricks.
Snoopy fired once and he fired twice
And that bloody Red Baron went spinning out of sight.
Ten, twenty, thirty, forty, fifty or more!
The bloody Red Baron was rollin' up the score!
Eighty men died trying to end that spree
Of the bloody Red Baron of Germany!

His first order of business was to find the right band, or singer, to record it. "Phil brought the song here for us," said Ronny Elliott. "From the time he started messin' with us and everything, he was always saying 'I've got this song that'll be the one. This'll be your hit.'"

He said the same thing about "Snoopy vs. the Red Baron," as it was now titled. It couldn't miss.

But the Outsiders-turned-Soul Trippers, already stung by the failure of "King Bee," suffered a major setback when their rhythm guitarist got a letter from the draft board, directing him to report for a physical exam, the first step of the induction process.

This caused him to quit the band in a panic, and in turn Laurie pulled them off the bill of an imminent European tour with the Chiffons and other label artists. The Soul Trippers called it a day.

Anyway, Elliott said, "I don't know if we would have done it with the Snoopy thing written into it. We were sure that we were far too hip for any such thing."

Gernhard, undaunted, went back to the Surfer's Club, where the Tropics were again rehearsing. He sat in a chair, holding his yellow paper, and sang "Snoopy vs. the Red Baron" for them.

They rejected it outright. "Too bubblegum-ish," said Souza. At that moment, the Tropics were the hottest thing in the Tampa-St. Pete area, and they played all over Florida, opening concerts for top national and international acts. In those days before it was called rock, the Tropics were a serious rock 'n' roll band. No way were they going to make a *novelty record*.

Gernhard then turned to the Royal Guardsmen, a band he'd just started working with at Charles Fuller Hunt's studio.

The Royal Guardsmen came from Ocala, about 100 miles north of Tampa, where four of the six musicians were still in high school.

The band included Chris Nunley on lead and harmony vocals, and occasional blues harmonica; lead singer and rhythm guitarist Barry Winslow; drummer John Burdett; bass player (and band founder) Bill Balogh; guitarist Tom Richards, whose family only had only recently moved from Tampa to Ocala; and baby-faced organist Billy Taylor, who'd joined the band just a month or so before their Tampa debut in the spring of '66.

Balough was a student at Central Florida Junior College; Nunley (at 20, the oldest Guardsman) was studying business at the University of Florida in nearby Gainesville.

The band's name was taken from the brand of guitar amplifier they used — Vox's Royal Guardsman model. Every day after school, they practiced on the back patio of guitarist Tom Richards' house. "We'd be wailing away into the pine trees until the police turned up to tell us to turn it down," Taylor laughed, "because the bank president next door, Mr. Thrift, was trying to get in his afternoon nap before he went back to the office."

If it rained, they moved the gear into the Richards' garage, and sometimes into the family dining room. "Although it gets noisy at times," Tom's mother told the *Ocala Star-Banner*, "I really enjoy it."

The Royal Guardsmen had been introduced to Tampa audiences by

21-year-old John Veciana, an employee at Ron's Record Shop in Tampa. It was the only place in the city to stock every single in the *Billboard* Top 100; Ron's was where the local musicians, who hoped to make records, hung out.

Veciana got the Ocala sextet a booking at the Spot, Tampa's top teen club. This led to further bookings — only on weekends, of course, and only when the impossibly young musicians could get rides to the big city to the south - and a minor buzz developed around the Royal Guardsmen.

Gernhard, who had a handshake arrangement with shop owner John Centinaro to book local dances, was a regular at Ron's. And he had a built-in buzz detector.

At their first Charles Fuller session, Gernhard had recorded the band playing an emotionally raw, soul-tinged Young Rascals ballad called "Baby Let's Wait," which was part of their live act.

He chose this one, with an almost tearful lead vocal from Barry Winslow, as the Guardsmen's first single. "Leaving Me," a percolating rocker with close-harmony vocals, became the flip side of the group's Laurie Records debut.

"Baby Let's Wait" was No. 1 in Ocala, the boys' hometown. Tampa radio played it, too, but it wasn't a hit. Nor did it get within spitting distance of the national charts.

As the single was beginning its slow rise to nowhere, the Guardsmen had been added to the bill of a Sunday afternoon rock 'n' roll show at Curtis Hixon Convention Hall in Tampa. Co-produced by Centinaro and Gernhard, the dance — with the flamboyant Monti Rock, from California, as the national headliner - was held in the Gasparilla Room, a large banquet facility in the Curtis Hixon complex.

"We were setting up our equipment, when Phil comes up holding his legal pad with these lyrics on it," recalled Chris Nunley. "He said he'd been shopping this song around to a bunch of different area groups. He wanted us to come up with some kind of treatment — there was a note in the corner that said 'simple, three or four chords, military feel on the snare drum.' He said 'We want to get different treatments and see which one turns out the best.'" Nunley, not all that interested, nodded and went back to what he'd been doing.

Next, Gernhard began talking quietly with Barry Winslow. He'd put out "Baby Let's Wait" as a single because he liked Barry's voice and thought it had "commercial potential," and he wanted Barry to take the lead on this new one.

Billy Taylor: "I remember Barry had a Baldwin guitar. There were seats around the edge of the Gasparilla Room, and Phil took him aside. They sat over there knee to knee while we set up. Phil tried to sing it; tried to give him the feel for the song."

Winslow put the sheet of paper into his guitar case. "I'll be up to see you in about 10 days," Gernhard told the band. "To hear what you come up with."

The after-school rehearsals continued on the patio outside Tom Richards' parents' house. Gernhard's deadline was fast approaching — and the Royal Guardsmen had all but forgotten about "Snoopy vs. the Red Baron."

"One day he called and said 'I'm getting in my car. I'm coming up to hear your version,'" recalled Taylor. "And that's when we all got inspired. It was like, thank God the Interstate isn't done yet - it was a three-hour trip from St. Pete to Ocala."

At first, Nunley said, "We didn't much like the song. We said 'Let's just do it real corny and real hokey, and he won't like it.'"

They played it with a straight march cadence, *hup two three four*, with Winslow singing lead. They considered it a joke and laughed all the way through it. Recalled Winslow: "We were a bunch of pie-eyed kids. We're a *rock* band, man, we don't do that candy stuff."

"Gernhard came to town and we played the song for him," Nunley continued. "He was over by the P.A. speaker, listening. A&R guys will get right in the speaker to hear everything. And he said 'Hmm! Play that again.' So we played it again and he said 'You know, I think we can do something with this. Maybe a couple of little changes.'"

"When he turned around after we played it again, he was flushed," said Taylor.

"We were surprised," said Burdett. "And within 10 minutes, Phil had contracts, literally on the dining room table at Tom's house."

With the underage Guardsmen's parents looking on, a deal was struck, making Gernhard the band's manager, publisher and record producer for a three-year period.

From that moment on, it was all about Snoopy and the German guy.

"At first, they couldn't believe I was serious," Gernhard reflected. "But when I finally convinced them I was serious, they got serious. It took me

A cool bunch of teens: Winslow, left, Taylor, Balogh, Nunley, Burdett and Richards. Laurie Records publicity photo.

two weeks to loosen them up enough to have fun with it the way they did at the audition."

The song was cut quickly at Fuller, with Charles Fuller Hunt's right-hand man, John Brumage, engineering. Hunt gave Gernhard the studio time and tape on spec — believing, as Phil did, that this record could be the one to take off. It was a fun session, because they were all thinking the same thing: What if?

"Our little studio did not have any high end audio stuff, so we sent everything 'dry' to the label," Brumage said. "The music track was created first, overdubbed a few times, then the vocals were layered on the second track. I seem to recall there are eight layers of overdubbing on 'Snoopy vs. the Red Baron.'"

Thinking back to the Holidays' unreleased original, from New Orleans, Gernhard overdubbed the sounds of a roaring plane engine, machine guns and explosions.

Still, it needed something — a memorable kickoff! It was Chris Nunley who suggested a loud burst of shouted "propaganda" in German; he just happened to be studying the language up at the University of Florida.

Achtung! Jetzt wir singen zusammen die Geschichte über den Schweinköpfigen Hund und den lieben Red Baron!

Which translates as:

Attention! We will now sing together the story of that pig-headed dog and the beloved Red Baron!

In the middle section of the recording, Gernhard had the Guardsmen abruptly change the time signature and insert several bars of "Hang on Sloopy," which had been a chart-topper in 1965 by the McCoys, a garage band from Indiana. But the Guardsmen instead sang "Hang on Snoopy, Snoopy hang on."

Before he finalized the master recording of "Snoopy vs. the Red Baron," Gernhard, probably anticipating a legal challenge down the road, wiped the vocals from this section. The "Hang on Sloopy" instrumental break remained.

Holler was tracked down in North Carolina, and he threw in his support. Adding Snoopy, he said, was a brilliant idea. He and Gernhard shared songwriting credit, even though the sections were written miles — and years — apart.

Laurie Records had put out "Baby Let's Wait," so they were offered first refusal on "Snoopy vs. the Red Baron."

"Phil told me that he showed the song to a lot of labels, and I'm not sure if that's true or not," Holler said. "Anyway, Laurie would've been far down the totem pole. Even at the time we went to them, everybody was suing them because they weren't getting paid. I think they were getting ready to declare bankruptcy."

Laurie's only hit that year had been the Chiffons' "Sweet Talkin' Guy" in May, and "Baby Let's Wait" didn't exactly set the world on fire. Still, the label could give the record national distribution and promotion, which would be necessary should it start to catch the ears of the country's kids.

Bob and Gene Schwartz were shrewd enough to see that Gernhard was on to something with "Snoopy vs. the Red Baron." And so they bought the master to the song, along with a throwaway original called "I Needed You" for placement on the B side.

But they also informed him that Charles M. Schulz, and United Features Syndicate, the distributor of *Peanuts*, would have to be consulted about the use of the Snoopy character. This had not occurred to Gernhard.

Dick Holler: "The lawyers said 'Here's what's gonna happen. If you put it out and it's a bomb, you've got nothing to worry about. They won't even write you a letter. If you put it out and it's a hit, that's good and it's bad.'

"They said 'The good thing is that you'll make some money, but the bad thing is that you're going to be giving some of it to them. Because it's a strict, open and shut copyright violation."

And there was another thing: The song's title was perilously close to that of Schulz's kiddie book, the 62-page *Snoopy and the Red Baron*.

Gernhard wrote the cartoonist a personal letter, flattering him and appealing to him to let Snoopy be a part of what was quite likely going to be a financial windfall for everybody.

But Schulz, as was his wont with such things, did not respond. Meanwhile, Gernhard and the Schwartz Brothers were on needles and pins.

Gernhard ordered Guardsmen Winslow and Nunley back to Tampa to record several lines of alternate vocals for the song.

Achtung! Jetzt wir singen zusammen die Geschichte über den Schweinköpfigen Amerikaner und den lieben Schwarzer Ritter!

Which translates as:

Attention! We will now sing together the story of that pig-headed American and the beloved Black Knight!

To play it safe, Snoopy, "a funny-looking dog with a big black nose" became Squeaky, "a buck-toothed beaver with a gleam in his eye." "The Bloody Red Baron" had been watered down to "Air Marshall Dummkopfen."

Laurie did a test run of the Royal Guardsmen's second single, "Squeaky vs. the Black Knight," in the remote climes of Canada.

It was also sent to select American radio stations, according to Dick Holler, just to see if anything happened. "Laurie had a whole system of DJs all over the country who would test records for 'em," he said. "A Payola scheme. They tested 'Squeaky vs. the Black Knight.' Nothing! It shipped cardboard. Nobody liked it."

Least of all Gernhard, who wasn't in the business of making buck-toothed beavers famous, thank you very much. And the Royal Guardsmen, a serious bunch of young musicians who'd only cut the "Snoopy" song because Gernhard had dangled the words "hit record" in front of them like a carrot.

Peanuts was almost subliminal in the way it blended laugh-out loud humor with allegories and warm life lessons, and that was why the strip — and Snoopy in particular — was so spectacularly popular.

"Squeaky vs. the Black Knight" wasn't subtle; it could've been the theme to a Saturday morning cartoon series.

In 1966, there were just three television networks. Kids and teens, out of necessity, watched the same programs as their friends, especially those that were aimed squarely at their desirable young demographic. Springtime had dropped the axe on kid-friendly favorites *The Munsters*, *The Addams Family* and *The Patty Duke Show* — silly stuff all. Things were changing.

September brought *Star Trek* — one of the first series that let young-sters know it was OK to be a nerd — and, significantly, *The Monkees*.

Taking a page from the Beatles' movies *A Hard Day's Night* and, more specifically, the cartoonish *Help!*, the creators of *The Monkees* cast four disparate actor/singers as a group of talented, ambitious, cute and funny rock 'n' roll musicians, living communally and struggling to make ends meet until they got that Big Break.

They could be every-teens, the garage band next door. Like boys everyone knew in school!

Of course, each Monday-night episode wrapped music around the wacky goings-on, and much to the surprise of the show's producers, the songs — written by the likes of Gerry Goffin and Carole King, Neil Diamond and Tommy Boyce & Bobby Hart, and impeccably arranged and produced — became bigger than the series itself.

Every day, talk in P.E. and around the water fountain was about the Monkees — the hilarious TV show, the groovy songs on the radio, and the fact that Micky, Mike, Davy and Peter seemed so real, so relate-able — just fun-loving kids trying to get ahead in a world ruled by all-too-serious, iron-fisted grown-ups.

The Monkees premiered Sept. 12, and was an immediate smash. On Oct. 27, CBS aired its third Peanuts special. *A Charlie Brown Christmas* had garnered good reviews (and, more importantly, substantial ratings) the year

before, as hard that spring's baseball-themed *Charlie Brown's All-Stars!*
And so Schulz and his production company were given the green light
for *It's the Great Pumpkin, Charlie Brown*, a Halloween special based, like
its predecessors, on scenes and situations right out of the comic strip.

Since 1966 was the year of Snoopy's dogfights with the Red Baron —
Schulz's picture book was selling briskly — it was only natural that the
cartoonist and his TV animators devote a lengthy section of *It's the Great
Pumpkin, Charlie Brown* to this storyline.

It's the Great Pumpkin became the schoolyard's next talked-about TV
show. The top record in the country was "Last Train to Clarksville" by
the Monkees.

And that's when Gernhard and Laurie Records finally unleashed
"Snoopy vs. the Red Baron" by the Royal Guardsmen, as Laurie 3366. The
second week in November, 1966.

Reaction was immediate and intense. "Most records get airplay in
all the minor areas first, and that'll force a major on it," said Winslow.
"Then the major starts playing it, and then it's a big deal. Well, this was
just the other way around. I heard WLS out of Chicago play it — we could
get that at night in Florida — they started playing it every hour on the
hour. Then every half hour. Then every 15 minutes. Then it was every 15
minutes back to back. And the minors had to jump through their own
britches to try to get ahold of it."

Balough, too, remembered those magic early spins on WLS. "First
time I remember hearing the song on the radio, we were coming back
from playing a fraternity party in Gainesville," he said. "It was like 2 in
the morning. 'Whoa, that's us! Damn!' It was like hitting you in the face."

Sandy Gernhard remembered an evening in November, after her
husband got home from another grueling day in law school. "He picked
me up and sat me on the kitchen counter, and said 'I've got something
to tell you ....' He was real quiet about it.

"I thought 'Oh God, somebody's died.'

"And Phil said 'I think we have a hit.'"

"Snoopy vs. the Red Baron" sold more than a million copies in its first
week. It sold more quickly than "Yellow Submarine" by the Beatles, "Paint
it Black" by the Rolling Stones or "Good Vibrations" by the Beach Boys.

Laurie Records had to sub-contract additional pressing plants to
meet the demand.

"It was within a month's time frame, literally, from the time we recorded this thing to the time it started to kick," Winslow explained. "We had record companies calling, Gernhard was all excited and of course, we were too. Here's a bunch of garage band kids with an amazing record on their hands and thrust into the world of big rock 'n' roll."

In Australia, "Snoopy vs. the Red Baron" spent five weeks at No. 1 (with the word "bloody," considered naughty in those days, bleeped out).

Sandy was able to quit her job at the bank.

Dick Holler, who was working in a hardware store in tiny Goldsboro, North Carolina ("it was only famous because Andy Griffith was from there") did his part to make the wheels spin. "I had some friends in radio and I took it right down there," he said. "They went on it right away. It was really cool.

"And I was a huge celebrity in that town because it only had about 30,000 people! The headline said LOCAL MAN WRITES HIT RECORD!"

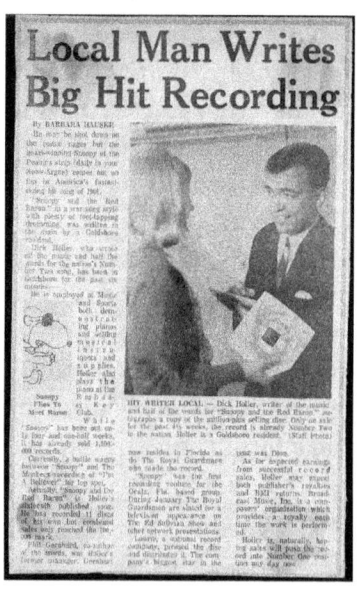

The story goes that Charles M. Schulz first became aware of the Royal Guardsmen record when a friend casually remarked, "That's a great song you wrote." The cartoonist fished out Gernhard's letter — which he apparently hadn't read — and called the United Features Syndicate lawyers.

The upper hand belonged to Schulz and his distributor. Had they not reached a financial agreement, a "Cease and Desist" injunction would have forced Laurie to pull the record.

But there was money to be made, without Schulz having to lift a finger. Gernhard pointed this out when he paid an emergency visit to the cartoonist's home in California, hat in hand.

In the end, according to Dick Holler, Schulz and his legal team demanded and were given a three-cent override, unheard of at the time.

That meant that for every "Snoopy vs. the Red Baron" 45 snatched up by hungry little hands (for around 89 cents a pop), Snoopy's creator was entitled to three cents. As one-half of the songwriting team, Holler received one-half cent per record. Gernhard, because he produced the single, co-wrote the song and was the de facto manager of the Royal Guardsmen, earned a penny and a half.

The Royal Guardsmen's cut was 3 percent of 90 percent of total record sales, which meant they were given 2.7 cents per record, split six ways.

On the last *Billboard* chart of the year, Dec. 31, 1966, "Snoopy vs. the Red Baron" was at No. 2, where it would spent a month lodged behind "I'm a Believer," the second single release from that unstoppable juggernaut, the Monkees, and go no further.

The band's official press photograph was taken at Six Gun Territory, Ocala's western-themed amusement park (Disney World, and the total annihilation of Florida's small-town theme park industry, wouldn't come until 1971).

High school students in 1966 were forbidden from growing their hair long; Barry Winslow and Tom Richards had been suspended from Ocala High that year until they got it cut to regulation length. In the photo, rule-breakers Winslow, Richards and Burdett (plus Billy Taylor, the youngest member of the band) wore women's wigs, procured by Gernhard and the musicians the night before from a local hairdresser's shop. The accommodating retailer let them come in and get fitted after closing time, so the potentially embarrassing task could be performed in secrecy.

The Royal Guardsmen couldn't capitalize on their success by touring the country until their Christmas holiday from school. Still, said Nunley, "We were flying high. We were just doing what they told us to do — load up, go here, go there." A string of package-show dates starring the Beach Boys, who'd just issued "Good Vibrations," lasted through Dec. 28 (the west coast dates also included, ironically, a band with the name Sopwith Camel).

Gernhard and Laurie rush-released an album by Christmas. Also titled *Snoopy vs. the Red Baron*, it was knocked out over 21 sweaty hours at the Fuller studio, with little to no editorial input from the band members themselves. Although the Royal Guardsmen's stage repertoire included the latest, hippest hits from the Beatles, the Stones and Paul Revere and the Raiders, Gernhard had drawn up a list of songs that he thought would work well alongside their novelty smash.

The band members hated the idea, but who were they to argue with success? So they rehearsed in Ocala, on Mr. and Mrs. Richards' backyard patio, and drove back down to Tampa to cut a half-dozen pop songs with comical cartoon or "kiddie" themes, including:

"Alley Oop," by the Hollywood Argyles, itself based on a comic strip;

"Little Red Riding Hood," a recent hit by Sam the Sham and the Pharaohs;

"The Jolly Green Giant," a bluesy parody by the Kingsmen of "Louie Louie" fame;

"Peanut Butter," a goofy adaptation of "Hully Gully" that both the Marathons and Chubby Checker had recorded;

"Road Runner," the Bo Diddley blues scorcher, which, despite its title, had nothing to do with the popular Warner Brothers cartoon;

"Bo Diddley," by Bo Diddley, which was always something of a children's song anyway.

One of the strangest cuts on the album was a talking comedy number called "Bears," which Nunley knew from a 45 in his collection, by an otherwise unheard-of Seattle band called The Fastest Group Alive.

(Brumage recalled recording a band member chewing a mouthful of potato chips on a very hot microphone to create the "bone crunching" sound effects on "Bears.")

Gernhard also had the group record a straightforward rendition of the Bacharach-David western drama "The Man Who Shot Liberty Valance," and, to connect the dots with the origins of the album's title song, Johnny Horton's "The Battle of New Orleans."

There was one original Guardsmen song, the poppy "Sweetmeats Slide," plus the already released A-sides "Baby Let's Wait" and, of course,

"Snoopy vs. the Red Baron."

Rejected at the last minute was the Coasters' 1959 novelty hit, "Charlie Brown." It was decided that Schulz would probably frown on this song about a less-than-lovable loser — definitely not his famous round-headed kid, Snoopy's master. No reason to make the cartoonist mad, after all.

This wasn't standard garage-band fare for 1966; in fact, pre-"Snoopy," only "Baby Let's Wait" had been a regular feature in the Guardsmen's live sets. They'd had to learn all the others, one song at a time.

"Snoopy," of course, would be played at every single live show they did for the rest of their lives.

"We were just given the songs and herded in there," said Billy Taylor. "But we practiced every day after school - even before the record stuff. It was just something the band wanted to do. We were a great cover band for the time. Very disciplined for our age group."

And no way was Schulz going to let Laurie use an image of Snoopy on the cover.

"That first album cover was a disaster that Laurie came up with,

one of the incredibly worst album covers you can imagine," laughed Dick Holler. "It showed the Baron as a grizzly old fat German guy with a moustache, flying a biplane. I told Gernhard 'Don't accept this, it's trash.' But the label persevered.

"And as a penalty for accepting that album cover, that album cover is still in the window of a display at the Smithsonian Air & Space Museum in Washington. All these years later! Every time I go by there, I say 'Gernhard, that's what you get, man, for allowing that crappy album cover.'"

Although the single made history, the *Snoopy vs. the Red Baron* album — crappy cover and all - did not get higher than No. 44. Starting in November, *The Monkees* would spend 13 weeks at No. 1, until it was knocked out of the spot by *More of the Monkees*, No. 1 for 18 weeks.

The Royal Guardsmen were frequent visitors to St. Petersburg, where they'd lounge around the office basking in the reflected glory of their new best buddy, the older (and worldly) Phil Gernhard.

"We'd go down to Phil's and work on business for a couple of hours," remembered Nunley. "Then he'd say 'Let's go to lunch!'"

"Nobody wanted to ride in Phil's car with him, because being a record producer he'd turn on the radio, after 10 seconds of a song he'd hit a button, change the station. Then another song, then hit a button. You'd say 'Hey, I like that song' and he'd just go 'Ehhhh …' and hit the button again."

Gernhard, meanwhile, was thinking about what they should do next. He was making it up as he went along.

Gernhard behind the board at Charles Fuller Hunt's studio.
Family photo.

6

Sopwith Camel Time

ST. PETERSBURG, Fla. — Phil Gernhard, a senior law student at Stetson College here, has formed Gernhard Enterprises, an independent production — publishing — management complex specializing in pop music. The publishing entity, SanPhil Music (BMI) has signed two exclusive writers, Dick Holler, who wrote "Snoopy vs. the Red Baron" with Gernhard, and John McCullough, who wrote "The Return of the Red Baron" with James McCullough and Gernhard.

Billboard
March 25, 1967

By definition, novelty records had a short shelf life, and striking while the proverbial iron was hot was paramount, before the kids who snapped up the first single moved on to some new craze.

Immediately following the success of "Snoopy vs. the Red Baron," Gernhard reached out to the accomplished songwriters in his orbit, asking them to create a sequel for him. The McCullough brothers sent down "The Return of the Red Baron," a virtual clone of the first song, which the Royal Guardsmen dutifully if unenthusiastically recorded at Fuller in early January.

*A bunch of clean-cut teens. Clockwise from left Winslow, Burdett, Balogh, Richards,
Nunley and Taylor. Laurie Records Publicity photo.*

Hey watch out little Snoopy
You're really in a mess
You through you were through with the bloody Red Baron
But it looks like he's not down yet

In February and March, the single competed for chart supremacy
against "Penny Lane" by the Beatles, "Ruby Tuesday" by the Rolling Stones,

the Turtles' "Happy Together" and the Left Banke's second hit, "Pretty Ballerina."

The Guardsmen and Gernhard cut a dozen additional songs — several of them composed by the young musicians themselves — at Fuller.

They were happy sessions, more relaxed than the rush job of the first album. They were all high on success and working together as a team.

"I'd be one of the first done with the tracks, laying down that initial track with the guys, and I'd go into the control room where Phil and John Brumage were, and Phil would always ask my opinion on certain things," Bill Balogh remembered. "I'm a novice — what do I know? But he was always nice like that."

Gone were the jokey cartoon songs aimed at small children. The second album contained state-of-the-art 1960s pop ("Any Wednesday," dripping with chiming 12-string guitar and rich vocal harmonies; the tuneful and bouncy "Airplane Song").

Conversely, the instrumental "Om" pureed organ, heavy drums and 12-string guitar together for a dreamlike, trippy ride through the Mystic East (a sitar would not have been out of place).

Defying categorization, "Searchin' For the Good Times" stole the drums-and-organ centerpiece of the Monkees' "I'm Not Your Steppin' Stone" and combined it with a Eastern European, minor-key melody - perhaps the first-ever klezmer pop song.

Dick Holler and Johnny McCullough shared writing credit on one of the album's cleverest pop songs. "Shot Down" — which had absolutely nothing to do with Snoopy or the Red Baron, despite the title — was the hit that never was.

Because of the money he was raking in, Gernhard was given a green light by Laurie to bring the master tapes to New York for embellishment. He was paired with composer John Abbott — the guy who wrote the faux-classical arrangements for the Left Banke — and together they added light strings, percussion and backup singers to the songs that would make up the second album, also to be called *The Return of the Red Baron*.

Although they'd been given more legroom, when it was time to track the final song for the album, they were reminded that Gernhard might have been a benevolent dictator, but he was still the boss:

"We were on a deadline," Nunley recalled. "We got the music cut for 'So You Want to Be a Rock 'n' Roll Star,' we did a scratch vocal, and Phil

Dick and Phil, cooking up another winner in the back room of Gernhard Enterprises' St. Petersburg office. Family photo.

said 'We don't have time to finish this — I've gotta get this tape up to New York.' So we never did the vocals."

And so the backing track for the Royal Guardsmen's version of the recent hit by the Byrds was released on their second album — as an instrumental.

Up in Andy Griffith's hometown, Holler was only too happy to take up Gernhard's invitation to move to St. Petersburg and work as a "staff writer." As for sharing the publishing on his songs with "SanPhil Music" — that was part of Phil's contract - he figured it was better than nothing.

McCullough, likewise, didn't have a lot going on.

People were in and out of Gernhard Enterprises' rented bungalow on First Avenue South in St. Petersburg day and night. Sandy, who sat at the reception desk, greeted a steady stream of local musicians who wanted to make records, songwriters pitching their latest to Mr. Gernhard, businessmen, record men, journalists, fans, and the occasional

Royal Guardsman, who'd slip into the back room where Holler worked at an upright Spinet piano.

Local DJ Charles "Charlie Brown" Troxell was ostensibly brought in to take over Royal Guardsmen management from Gernhard. That was his job title, although what was really doing was hanging around the office because Phil and Sandy liked him.

As the second Guardsmen album languished in the lower regions of the chart, the "Return of the Red Baron" single made it to No. 15 — not exactly a smash, but a reasonable showing, and enough to keep them on the label. Laurie issued both "Airplane Song" and "Any Wednesday" as followup singles, but each in its turn died a death in that summer of flower power and *Sgt. Pepper's Lonely Hearts Club Band*.

Despite their best efforts, the Royal Guardsmen could not escape the "Snoopy" choke-chain.

The boys let their guard down — just a little - in a lengthy interview given to the British paper *New Musical Express*:

Barry Winslow: *"The dog's very hip and happening right now, but let's not kill him off by over-exposure."*

Tom Richards: *"What we have to do now and in the future is destroy the 'novelty' tag we're getting as a result. We can't wait till our summer school break so we can get down to some really serious work on a new album."*

John Burdett: *"We don't believe we can be the real Muddy Waters or Jimmy Reed type R&B act, but we're certain that with enough experimentation, we can come up with something acceptable, new, unusual and, we hope, identifiable with us as a unit."*

On May 3 Phil and Sandy, accompanied by Dick Holler, attended the annual BMI awards dinner at the swanky Hotel Pierre in New York City. "Snoopy vs. the Red Baron" was officially one of the most-played songs of 1966.

The youngest Guardsmen graduated from high school in June, and almost immediately the band embarked on a cross-country package tour, 70 shows in 60 days. They were bottom of the bill on the "Summer Shower of Stars," after Tommy James and the Shondells, Keith (of "98.6" fame) and the Sam The Sham Revue.

Sam "Wooly Bully" Samudio was trying to shake his campy image, and so his group — still called the Pharaohs, for continuity's sake — had traded their robes and turbans for stylish corduroy suits. The Revue also

The "Summer Shower of Stars" cross-country tour, 1967, with Tommy James & the Shondells, the Sam the Sham Revue and Keith. Tommy James is at center with his arms out; the Royal Guardsmen (with road manager Charles Troxell) are standing at far left. Laurie Records.

included "The Shamettes," a trio of comely female backup singers. They'd morphed into an R&B show band, kind of a white Ike & Tuna Turner.

Everyone traveled together in an air-conditioned private coach. In this environment, the Royal Guardsmen, famous for their kiddie novelty songs, felt like rock 'n' roll charlatans. Their "entourage" consisted of Charles Troxell and Johnny McCullough, who helped to set up the equipment at each county fair and American Legion Hall, but were essentially there to serve as chaperones at the insistence of the boys' parents. Troxell, with his booming DJ voice, also served as the "emcee," introducing all the acts at the shows.

Privately, the boys began to refer to themselves as the NSB — the National Shit Band.

"We were the openers on the tour, and so we tested the equipment for everybody else," Nunley said. "And if it went bad, we sounded like shit. So, National Shit Band."

Taylor said they used the alter ego as a release valve, to remind themselves not to take everything so seriously. "We were going to break up and regroup as the National Shit Band," he laughed. "Tom even drew up a logo."

The May 6 issue of *Billboard* included a small item announcing a Houston, Texas satellite office for Gernhard Enterprises. Stan Hardin — McCullough's old cohort from Columbia and the Archers - would be Gernhard's Texas talent scout, with sessions held at Jones Recording, "which is equipped with 8-track facilities."

Gernhard told the magazine there was an abundance of "pop writing and talent" in the Houston area, which could contribute to what he called — without explanation - the "Southern Pop Sound."

This was another example of Phil's gift for blowing smoke and hyperbole into the air. The sole fruits of the Texas endeavor would appear in the fall, a Gernhard-produced single on Decca called "Houdini," by the pop band The Dream Machine — published, of course, by SanPhil Music.

It was a sappy song and an undistinguished recording, with nothing particularly "Southern" about it.

At the conclusion of the Summer Shower of Stars tour, the Guardsmen and their producer re-convened at the Fuller studio.

The first song presented to the band was, predictably, another shaggy dog story. The Guardsmen wanted to break that mold. "We were pissed off at Gernhard and the record company," said Nunley. "They wouldn't do anything. Gernhard just kept saying 'My hands are tied.' The Schwartzes just said 'More Snoopy.'"

"Snoopy's Christmas" was written by the Tin Pan Alley songwriting team known as Hugo & Luigi, with their frequent collaborator George David Weiss (the trio had composed Elvis Presley's "Can't Help Falling in Love," among others, and were working at the time on the Broadway musical *Maggie Flynn*). Hugo (Peretti) and Luigi (Creatore) kept an office in the legendary center of New York's pop music universe, the Brill Building.

Holler, who'd moved his family to Florida, wasn't happy. "They sent it down to us originally, but I re-wrote it, I arranged it and Phil and I produced it," he said. "The label, who were nothing but a bunch of crooks, said 'Oh, Hugo & Luigi don't allow any co-writers on their songs.' They were typical, as David Letterman liked to say, record company weasels."

Holler was given the B-side, as a sort of consolation prize, for his song "It Kinda Looks Like Christmas."

"Snoopy's Christmas" was (very loosely) based on a real incident from World War I, a Christmas Day truce between British and German soldiers.

In the Hugo & Luigi version, the Red Baron again shoots our hero down —
but instead of finishing him, he offers a cheery toast: "Merry Christmas,
mein friend," leaving Snoopy, filled with the sentimental spirit of the
season, to fight another day.

Studio owner Charles Fuller Hunt bought a celesta — a tiny, piano-like
keyboard that makes a melodic tinkling sound — so Billy Taylor could
play it on the Christmas song.

Next, the Guardsmen were flown to New York City, where they were
booked into Allegro Recording Studios — located in the basement of
the Brill Building, where the tape machine had to be stopped whenever
a subway train roared by — to finish the single, and track their third
album.

Thrilled to leave the tiny Fuller facility behind, the Guardsmen looked
forward to working in what was a "real" studio, with eight tracks to play
with, and in the Big Apple to boot!

"Phil was great in the studio," Burdett said. "During the 'Snoopy's
Christmas' recordings in New York, the conductor of the orchestra said
my drum cadence changes after the intro, and he didn't like it. Phil said
to him, 'That's the way it is, it's worked in the past.' The conductor walked
out; we and the members of the orchestra were not unhappy.

"I really wanted to have tympani in 'Snoopy's Christmas.' Phil took
the time to let me record them. I never heard them in the song, but that
was OK."

"Snoopy's Christmas" was an enormous hit. It sold more than a million copies in 1967 alone, and was No. 1 on a special *Billboard* chart
called "Best Bets For Christmas." Once again, the band topped the (regular) charts in Australia. In New Zealand, it was the year's fastest-selling
non-domestic single, ultimately moving more than 100,000 units.

The album, which was to be called *Snoopy and His Friends,* would only
include five new Royal Guardsmen songs, all on Side Two. Gernhard and
the Schwartz Brothers had cooked up an elaborate marketing plan for
their 1967 Christmas release.

Gernhard and Holler wrote three short voice-over narrations, in the
form of radio news bulletins describing the action in the German skies
as von Richthofen and his "Flying Circus" terrorized the flyboys of the
British RAF. Voice actor Larry Foster provided the characters' British,
French, German and Australian accents, with battlefield sounds blasting

away in the background. These were played straight, with no mention of a cartoon beagle on a flying doghouse.

Never mind that such broadcasts did not exist in the years of World War I. This was fantasy, after all.

Each "news bulletin from the front lines" led directly into one of the Royal Guardsmen's already-released Snoopy songs, with "Snoopy's Christmas" — the current hit, or "money" track - as the final entry in the Side One trilogy.

Along with his holiday tune, Holler contributed the rocking "Down Behind the Lines," a love story with a vague fighter-pilot storyline, and a bubblegum pop tune called "Sopwith Camel Time," his first-ever composition directed squarely at the Royal Guardsmen's core audience:

All of the week, I'm workin' so hard
Doin' my homework, rakin' the yard

Listening to a playback of "Snoopy's Christmas" at Allegro Studios in New York, 1967. Standing from left: Arranger John Abbott, Dick Holler, Royal Guardsmen John Burdett, Barry Winslow, Tom Richards, Billy Taylor and Chris Nunley. Seated from left, are: Laurie Records chief Gene Schwartz, Phil Gernhard and engineer Bruce Hamper. Laurie Records.

Just hangin' on till Friday at three
Then it's down to the runway for me.
'Cause it's Sopwith Camel time!
Sopwith Camel Time!

The upgrade in sound quality was noticeable — Gernhard, Abbott and co-producer Holler made full use of Allegro's eight-track palette.

Writing together, Guardsmen Taylor and Winslow contributed a strong pop composition, "I Say Love," which Abbott and Gernhard tastefully embellished with a gentle flute, and a light, Caribbean tropical touch of female singers in the background (it would become the album's second single early in 1968). "So Right (to Be in Love)," also written by Taylor and Winslow, was a jaunty "sunshine pop" number that recalled their heroes, the Young Rascals.

"Phil tried to please us with the releases," said Burdett, "but I think that's all he was doing, in a bid to keep us doing more Snoopy."

But Gernhard wasn't finished. He'd persuaded Schulz — who finally understood the PR value - to give them an image of Snoopy, standing in repose by his doghouse, as the front cover. And the cartoonist even drew in little caricatures of the six Royal Guardsmen, each sporting scarves and goggles, peering out from behind Snoopy's domicile.

Historically, Schulz rarely drew "real" people, so it was a real coup for Gernhard Enterprises, Laurie Records and the six kids from Ocala.

Attached to the back cover was a tear-away poster, also designed by Schulz, with a cartoon showing the dog of the hour dressed in a red sleeping gown and cap, encircled by a green wreath festooned with red and blue lights. At the top, it said "Merry Snoopy Christmas."

Endorsed at long last!

"I think Schulz's people probably got on his ass," Holler said, "and said 'Hey man, these people are working hard with your stupid dog, and you're not even letting them use old footage.' And so Schulz agreed to let them use Snoopy on the doghouse, and then he actually drew those caricatures of the boys.

"So we thought well, Schulz at least realizes that we're in the business and we're serious. And we're making him money."

The Schulz-illustrated album jacket, according to Taylor, "was news to us. Gernhard might have mentioned it, but it was nothing I remember ever being discussed, or presented to us for a vote.

"Often he would be talking, and then he would just throw out something like 'Oh, Schulz is going to do the cover.' That was the way he passed on information. I don't think he was trying to rock our world or anything, I think it just popped into his head because he had so much on his mind, and his mind went in many different directions."

The band embarked on a 10-city tour, with Tommy James and the Shondells, on Dec. 10. Each show was a "Toys For Tots" benefit, with 20,000 plush Snoopy dolls to be given away as the group visited children's hospitals and orphanages in each city.

In Philadelphia, they performed on *The Mike Douglas Show*, lip-synching to "Snoopy vs. the Red Baron," "I Say Love" and "Snoopy's Christmas." In New York, they taped an appearance on *The Joey Bishop Show*.

Gernhard, for his part, finally gave up on law school. He was simply too busy (and too successful) to go to class. Even the old man couldn't argue with his cash flow.

On Dec. 27, the *Tampa Tribune* published a profile of Gernhard, reporting that the "Snoopy's Christmas" single had passed one million in sales. Clutching his ever-present Tiparillo, the 26-year-old show business wizard puffed and pontificated, and discussed the future of Gernhard Enterprises, including "a semi-documentary film to be made about a 'Flower Child'" and the promotion of a Tampa appearance by Ray Charles — one of his heroes - come April.

"We are trying to develop a new industry in Florida," he explained. "With the Disney attraction coming and the Ivan Tors studios here, there is no reason St. Petersburg cannot become another New York or Memphis or Nashville or New Orleans of the recording industry."

And what of the Royal Guardsmen? "You have," Gernhard intoned portentously, "probably heard the last Snoopy and Red Baron record."

Can You Tell Me Where He's Gone

"The way you produce a record is you hear a song, and at the same time you hear something in your head. You use all your technical skill, and skill with people, trying to come up with this thing you hear in your head."

Phil Gernhard

Like the others on Gernhard's payroll, Carl "Charlie Brown" Troxell had his ears to the ground. He haunted the teen clubs, listening out for fresh new talent — or a talented band that could be molded to Gernhard's will - to take to the boss.

Troxell was hearing good things about a local group called the Beau Heems. When they landed an opening spot for the Royal Guardsmen at Tampa teen club the Inn Crowd, he caught their act. As it happened, Guardsmen guitarist Tom Richards' father, Olin, was already friendly with Tampa plumber Bill Carson, whose son — 15-year-old Bill Jr. — was the Beau Heems' drummer. So it was old-home night.

Fronted by 21-year-old Howard "Hoppi" Symans on vocals, the band had a rough, primitive sound — almost as "dirty" as the Outsiders — and Troxell believed they were unique enough to recommend to Gernhard. Keyboard player Dickie Barrett sat behind a massive Hammond B3 organ, with the requisite revolving Leslie speaker cabinet. Not every garage band could afford one of those.

When he saw them, Gernhard could hear the possibilities. After convincing the band to enlarge its name to the "more commercial" Hoppi and the Beau Heems, he quickly arranged a two-single deal with Laurie.

He promptly took them into Fuller and had them record "I Missed My Cloud," which he had knocked out one January afternoon with Johnny McCullough. Like many of Gernhard's lesser efforts, the record was a fairly obvious second generation clone of someone else's success: In this case, the Rolling Stones' "Get Off My Cloud," the point driven home with Symons' sneering, Mick Jagger-esque lead vocal. The melody (and prominent organ) was similar to "96 Tears," a recent hit by a band called ? and the Mysterians.

"Hey, getting a national record deal?" said Bill Carson Jr., laughing

With the first flush of "Snoopy" money, Phil bought a brand-new '68 Oldsmobile Toronado. A bumper sticker in back read "We're in. Let's win." Photo by Chris Nunley.

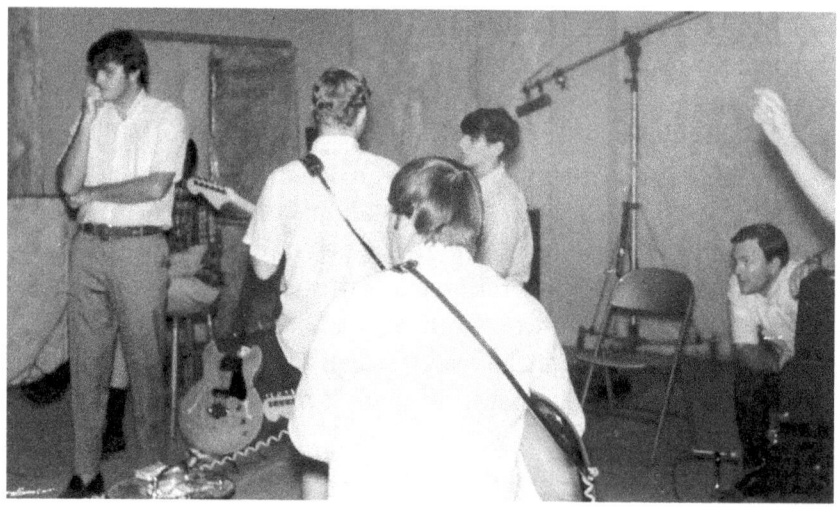

At Charles Fuller Productions in Tampa, Gernhard (seated at right) produces Hoppi and the Beau Heems' version of his song "I Missed My Cloud." From the collection of William Carson.

at the memory of the Beau Heems' derivative debut. "We would've done the Star-Spangled Banner."

The second single, a Symons original called "When I Get Home," sounded nothing like its predecessor. The B3 had turned into something dark and sinister, the sort of organ music kids were hearing on records by the Doors — one of the biggest bands of the era.

The faux Jagger of "I Missed My Cloud" was gone. Symons sang "When I Get Home" as a booming, theatrical, oversized Jim Morrison impression, right down to the anguished baritone cries of "Yeeeeeaah!" during the minor-key instrumental breaks.

Although the Beau Heems singles got the usual airplay from local stations, they did not break nationally, and the group's Laurie contract was not extended.

His coffers still plentiful with Snoopy money, Gernhard continued to poke and prod for his Next Big Thing. He caught the scent of The Raven, which Charles Fuller Hunt himself had already produced, and their song "Calamity Jane." Gernhard negotiated a low-risk, one-disc deal for The Raven on Rust Records, a Laurie subsidiary that had taken chances on two or three of his Briarwood masters.

"Calamity Jane" was an urgent, pleading pop song, embellished by

Gernhard with fuzzed-out Yardbirds guitar, an evocative organ solo, Morse-code sound effects, horns, sitar, flutes, cowbell and the unsettling ricochet of rifle shots.

Improbably, "Calamity Jane" would be one of Gernhard's greatest audio achievements. Like "Stay" and "Snoopy vs. the Red Baron," it is that rare bird, the perfect pop single.

Owing melodic nods to other great singles of the era, including the Association's "Along Comes Mary" and the American Breed's "Bend Me Shape Me," it was two minutes and three seconds of fiery garage band intensity, almost a "Wall of Sound" worthy of Phil Spector.

It did not, however, set the world on fire. "Calamity Jane" was a hit in Tampa and St. Petersburg — and, strangely, in Cedar Rapids, Iowa, where it reached No. 1 on the local hit parade — but America and the world at large gave it a pass. The Raven never cut another record and disappeared, like so many before them, into the ether.

Gernhard Enterprises entered the concert promotion business in April, with a highly publicized appearance by Ray Charles — one of Phil's idols — in Curtis Hixon Hall's 7,000-seat arena.

The concert promoter puts up the money to bring a performer on tour to his area. He books the hall, pays for marketing and publicity, and arranges the distribution of tickets.

The financial risk is all on the promoter's shoulders. The artist is guaranteed a certain amount; if not enough tickets are sold, the show loses money but the artist still has to be paid.

Conversely, if the concert is a success, the promoter makes a decent profit.

Gernhard had hired Ronny Elliott, the affable bass player from the Outsiders (and, by default, the Soul Trippers) to serve as his "ears" in the teen clubs. Elliott was also tasked with seeking out talent, and bringing the groups back to Gernhard.

"It was me and Dick and Johnny McCullough, and on the periphery there was also Kent LaVoie, Danny Finley and other people who were sort of in and out, depending on the time," Elliott said. "Our jobs were basically 'Bring me stuff I can make hit records with. With me, the idea was 'You're a kid, so you can tell the stuff I can't.' I was 19. He was like a grownup and I was not.

"But there was this built-in hitch: If I took him something good, it made him mad and he was jealous. If I didn't take him anything good, I wasn't doing my job."

The concert promotion business, Elliott explained, "always fascinated him. And honestly I think what caused him to go at it big time was, he resented giving me a salary and me having nothing to do most of the time. It wasn't my fault! I'd bring him stuff and he'd pass on it.

"By the time that I began to realize that Phil's ego wasn't going to allow any of my artists to even record, we were both frustrated. He was paying me a hundred bucks a week and neither of us was getting anything out of it. So I became the chief gopher to promote all these concerts." Gernhard later explained that promoting concerts, for him, was merely a way of making sure the rock artists he liked, that he wanted to see, came to town. According to Elliott, nearly every show presented by

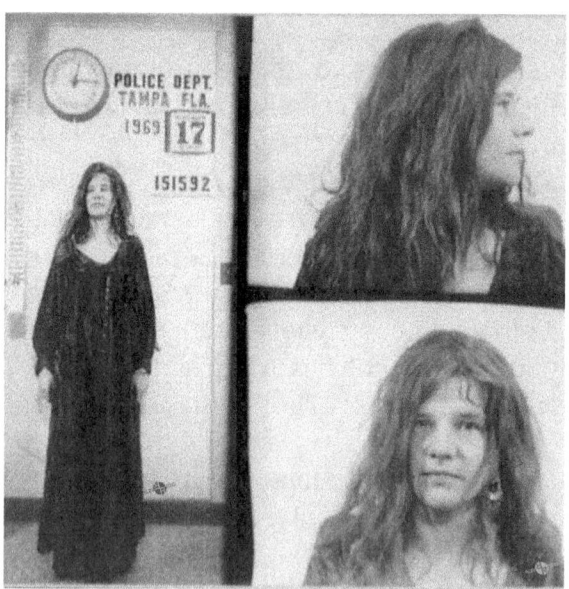

Nov. 17, 1969: Janis Joplin is arrested for shouting obscenities after a Gernhard-produced concert in Tampa. Phil bailed her out. Wikipedia.

Gernhard Enterprises — from Donovan to Creedence Clearwater Revival to Elton John — lost money.

But Gernhard, who enjoyed the attention lavished on him, kept at it. He liked being the guy who delivered the hottest, hippest acts, including Jimi Hendrix (twice) and Janis Joplin, who was famously arrested for shouting obscenities at a police officer from the stage of Curtis Hixon Hall. Phil personally bailed Joplin out of the Hillsborough County Jail.

"Anybody like Joplin, who was making ten grand for one night's work, should have some responsibility to the people who are paying her," he later complained to the *St. Petersburg Times*. "But she encouraged the kids to start tearing the place up, then came around demanding her money. The kids take it out on the greedy promoter. I feel sorry for anyone trying to promote rock concerts nowadays."

Meanwhile, tensions were mounting in the Royal Guardsmen camp, as every one of their non-"Snoopy" singles had failed miserably. Royalty checks were few, far between and inevitably skimpy. SanPhil Music controlled the publishing on the band's own compositions, and Gernhard did not open his company's books for the teenaged musicians to inspect.

Barry Winslow was the lead singer on the "Snoopy" numbers, and on all the other songs released as singles, too. The other band members had overheard Gernhard bragging about Winslow: "This kid's going to make me a million dollars." So they began to needle their lead singer, calling him the MDK — the Million Dollar Kid.

In the spring of 1968, Winslow quit the band. Like all healthy young American men, the draft dangled over his head like a guillotine ready to drop. Because he was out of high school, with no college deferment, he thought he was about to be called up. So he panicked, and set out to re-arrange (what was left of) his young life.

He kept in touch with Gernhard, however, and still drove down to St. Petersburg on weekends, to hang around the office, chat with Sandy and listen to Holler try out his new tunes in the back room. Music remained Winslow's first love.

The presidential primaries were in full swing, which gave Gernhard another idea. They were still in Schulz's good graces, despite their ever-decreasing record sales, and so a fourth "Snoopy" single was proposed. This time, the intrepid hound would make a run for the White House ... with the deciding vote, coming at the very last minute, cast by the Red

Baron himself.

Sure, it wasn't "MacArthur Park," but if they could just ride the political wave that was sweeping the country ... Holler and Gernhard dashed off "Snoopy For President" and booked Allegro for fresh Royal Guardsmen sessions — including a fourth album.

With high school out of the way, the band was free to travel on short tours as time allowed. With Barry sidelined by fears of imminent induction, they played a few previously-arranged dates as a quintet. Tom Richards' parents, Olin and June, traveled in the big Dodge van serving as managers and peace-keepers.

"We were on the road when Gernhard and the record company had this idea," Taylor recalled. "Olin came in and told us Barry was going to sing the songs, and they would use studio musicians. We would get our royalties as normal, even though we weren't playing."

Gernhard, it appeared, intended to make a star out of the Million Dollar Kid. Was this his plan all along?

"I would imagine it would be simple to manage one person," said Burdett. "The MDK was and still is the most vocally talented man I know. If anybody deserved stardom, it would be Barry."

"By that time," added Taylor, "a lot of negative attitude had begun to shift in. We knew we weren't gonna get to do anything serious, so we said 'Bring it on.' I don't think it probably meant a lot of financial gain for us."

The single was recorded first, using, as promised, studio musicians. Gernhard again cooked up a "gimmicky" intro — a radio announcement, a la the Christmas album, with a German-accented news announcer rattling off the names of the candidates then in the race for the White House ... *"President, United States, Kennedy, Nixon, McCarthy und Rockefeller, Schnoopy, Humphrey .... Schnoopy? Ach du lieber meine!..."*

The single was released late in May, in advance of the still-unfinished album.

Snoopy For President bears little resemblance to the other Royal Guardsmen albums. For one thing, there are no original compositions on it, and only the title song bore the familiar names of that famous songwriting team, Gernhard and Holler.

The rest were divided between tepid rock covers (the Fireballs' "Bottle of Wine," a medley of the Box Tops' "Cry Like a Baby" and "The Letter," Georgie Fame's campy "Bonnie and Clyde"), saccharine pop ballads of the day ("Honey," "By the Time I Get to Phoenix") and latter-day bubblegum hits ("Simon Says," "Yummy Yummy Yummy.")

Gernhard had discovered the lilting, country-ish folk song "Biplane 'Evermore'" on an Irish Rovers album earlier in the year, and had Winslow record it to provide a tenuous link to the band's earlier airplane-related titles. It's pleasant but not particularly memorable. It's the least grating thing on a decidedly grating longplayer.

It's likely that the Schwartz Brothers had demanded a more commercial set than *Snoopy and His Friends*, with its faux-news bulletins, so Gernhard pulled out all the stops.

Slick, polished — and almost totally without substance — *Snoopy For President* was just undistinguished 1968 pop, like so many others, without identity. A Barry Winslow solo album, disguised as the Royal Guardsmen, it could have been anybody.

"We felt slighted, but relieved we didn't have to record," said Burdett. "Probably the way the Monkees must have felt. Playing live and recording was often a real timing issue."

Holler and Gernhard were in New York the first week of June, polishing the final LP tracks with John Abbott. "It's a three or four-day project, so we're at a hotel," Holler recalled. "I'm asleep, and Phil comes in. He says wake up, they just shot Bobby."

Presidential candidate Robert F. Kennedy had been assassinated in Los Angeles.

"We turn on the television and we stay up for a pretty long time. Then we decide to cancel the session and go back home to St. Petersburg."

Laurie Records was forced to withdraw the "Snoopy for President" single, which been gaining momentum at radio. The spoken intro naming the presidential candidates — including Kennedy — was excised.

By the time the 45 was re-serviced to radio and retail, nobody was in the mood. And the album, even though Schulz had provided another Snoopy image for the cover, was likewise stillborn.

Back home in Florida, "We didn't really feel like working, but Phil said

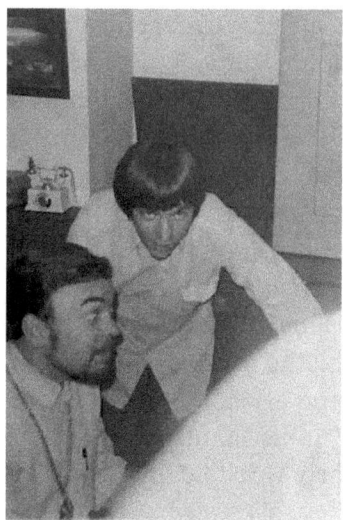

Holler runs through his latest composition, "Abraham, Martin and John," for Royal Guardsman Barry Winslow. Family photo.

'Let's go in and check our calls,'" said Holler. "The first day, I went into the back room and I wrote 'Abraham, Martin and John' in about 15 minutes. I did a treatment like the Kingston Trio might do it."

Holler's song paid tribute to Abraham Lincoln, John F. Kennedy, Martin Luther King Jr. and, just when you thought the song was over, the recently-murdered Bobby. (No one minded that the names were not in sequence, as "Abraham, John and Martin" didn't exactly roll off the tongue.)

Anybody here seen my old friend Abraham?
Can you tell me where he's gone?
He freed a lot of people, but the good die young
I just looked around, and he's gone.

"Abraham, Martin and John" would be a game-changer — for Holler, for Gernhard, even for the Royal Guardsmen.

Somehow Winslow had managed to avoid the draft, and was about the re-join the Guardsmen for a series of late-summer dates.

After the failure of "Snoopy For President," Laurie had re-released "Baby Let's Wait," the band's very first single, and it was getting some attention.

The band members, for their part, were grateful for anything that didn't have "Snoopy" in the title.

"The real turning point for me was when I drove down to St. Pete, from Ocala, to work with Dick on some demos," Winslow said. "I liked working with him, because I wanted to learn more about writing myself. Dick was playing his little upright, out-of-tune piano, and he was singing this little 6/8 shuffle: *Anybody here seen my old friend Abraham?* And I am just dying. I said 'This is cool! This is a really of-the-times song, man, but can we do it 4/4?' And Dick's getting into it — 'Yeah, this works good.'

"And Gernhard's in the other office. I said 'Phil, we need this song. The Guardsmen need this song. This will bust us loose. We love the puppy, but this may give us a real, legitimate shot.' He said 'Yeah, you guys can have it! But go ahead and cut it the way Dick's doing it, the 6/8 thing.' So we did it, a little piano, guitar and me on a little two-track Wizard machine. I was loving it. I said 'Wait till I tell the guys!'"

Gernhard and Holler spent a month trying out singers for "Abraham, Martin and John." Even Carl "Charlie Brown" Troxell was given an audition. Laurie Records artist Hank Cardell cut a spec version. Still, Gernhard wasn't hearing what we was looking for.

"We thought about getting the proper representation for the song, and making sure it was reverent enough," Holler said. "We didn't want to just throw it to anybody."

Then Laurie boss Gene Schwartz asked Gernhard to do him a favor. The label's top-selling artist was in a serious slump, both commercially and personally. New Yorker Dion DiMucci — whose career at Laurie had started in the late 1950s as the lead singer of Dion and the Belmonts, with "A Teenager in Love" and "Where or When" — had fallen on hard times. After solo hits with "The Wanderer" and "Runaround Sue," his career had been washed away by the cultural tsunami of the British Invasion, and in an instant Dion (as he was professionally known) was a has-been.

By 1968, he was a recovering heroin addict - and a newly-minted, born-again Christian - playing acoustic guitar for short pay in South Florida folkie clubs. Laurie's head of A&R, Doug Morris, promised the label's one-time golden boy they'd re-sign him, if he came up with the right song.

And so Gernhard and Holler took "Abraham, Martin and John" to the fallen star.

"We went down and saw him in Hialeah, in a little place out by the racetrack," Holler said. "He had just gotten out of rehab, so we didn't know what to expect. We were certainly worried about it. But other than being extremely shy and nervous about performing again, he still sang well. It struck Phil and me that his voice was still extraordinary. His druggie days hadn't taken that away from him."

Recalled Gernhard: "He was doing all these folk songs for me. Some he wrote, some were by Nilsson, Leonard Cohen ... he had a very mumbly kind of style. I thought, oh my God, this guy's voice is perfect for that song, because he won't telegraph it.

"I said 'I'm going to send you a song, and I want you to work it up in this same style. The writer's version is bouncy."

According to Gernhard, DiMucci insisted he didn't like "Abraham, Martin and John," and adamantly refused to record it. "His wife talked him into working it up with guitar and vocal ... perfect," Gernhard said. "He said 'I don't want to cut it.' I said I'll fly you to New York; all you have to do is sing it one time. It'll all be done before you get there.' I told him it's a free trip, you can go to the Bronx and see your friends."

In his memoir *The Wanderer: Dion's Story*, DiMucci said he thought "Abraham," on first listen, was "opportunistic" and distasteful. "I don't know why, but when I picked up a gut-string guitar and started putting it together, I started seeing the song differently ... as a three-minute piece of hope.

"It was a real restless time in the country then. These senseless assassinations seemingly took the hope out of people, but here was this song that said 'You can kill the dreamer, but not the dream: People are going to carry it on."

A week later in St. Petersburg, Barry Winslow, down from Ocala, strolled through the front door of the Gernhard Enterprises office. "I walk in the hall and there's Dion DiMucci," Winslow said. "He was real clammy and looked horrible when I met him; he was braced up against a wall, sitting on a stool. And Gernhard's just drooling all over him, you know?

"I walked into the kitchenette and I heard him: '*Anybody here* ....' And I'm thinking oh my God, he's done it. He's gonna give this to Dion. We are screwed.

"When he left, I just came unglued. I yelled at Gernhard and made a real scene. And that was pretty much it for me."

Undaunted, Gernhard — with the full support of the Schwartz Brothers and Morris — made good on his promise and flew Dion from Florida to New York. Session time had been booked at Allegro.

"I knew once I got him in the studio, there'd be no problem," Gernhard explained. "And he came in, played guitar and sang, and as I was listening to the playback, I had him punch in one line to correct it. He left. He did one take! That was the deal. He was gone."

John Abbott's arrangement for "Abraham, Martin and John" was lush, almost saccharine, with full orchestra, a lone, melancholy oboe, and most memorably, the sound of an angelic harp running between nearly every line of lyrics.

Maudlin? Certainly. But it was undeniably moving. This was a record designed to get your attention and focus it on the tragedy of America's murdered leaders.

Gernhard mixed the single in 20 minutes. "I wanted a very subliminal record, that wouldn't make any entreaty to cry," he explained.

He said it had come out the way he'd heard it in his head back in June — subtle, but impossible to forget. "It was the record I wanted. I didn't want them to understand it until the fourth or fifth listening."

It didn't take off right away. A DJ friend of Dick Holler's said the Dion single was *too* subtle. "You know, Dick," he'd said, "you've got a really good song here, but you can't understand what this record's about. It's not going to work."

Holler complained to Gernhard. "You made a record nobody can understand," the composer told the producer. "This is terrible."

Gernhard hung up the phone and put his head in his hands. "Christ, this is awful," he thought.

"Four days later, boom. Orders from everywhere."

"Abraham, Martin and John" sold a million records, reached No. 4 on the *Billboard* singles chart, and resuscitated Dion DiMucci's career.

And Phil Gernhard, who assigned himself half-ownership of the song's publishing, got richer.

"I don't want to brag," reflected Holler, "but 'Abraham, Martin and John' got Phil off the snide of being Mr. Novelty. I represented the publishing company on several trips to New York, and a lot of people wouldn't take us seriously because all we were doing was 'Snoopy,' and our other songs were songs like 'The Airplane Song' and 'Bye Bye Biplane,' all these teeny-bopper songs. So we didn't get too much respect."

The Smothers Brothers Comedy Hour, CBS, Sunday, Nov. 17, 1968:

Tom Smothers: "We first heard this next song on the radio, and we thought so much of it, we thought it was such a great song, we thought we'd like to have it on the show so that more people could hear it and see it performed."

Dick Smothers: "That's right. The song is entitled 'Abraham, Martin and John.' And we're very proud to present the man who has this hit record — ladies and gentlemen, Dionne!"

Smothers pronounced Dion's name de-*YON*, like he was an effeminate fashion designer, and coupled it with a theatrical hand flourish, as if the brothers were bringing out an opera star or some great maestro.

The idea, clearly, was not to tip off the viewers that this was Dion (*DEE*-yon), the washed-up teen star of "Runaround Sue" fame.

Dion performed it live with the same gut-string acoustic guitar he'd used on the recording. Because of a musicians' strike, the Smothers Brothers' orchestra was absent when this episode was taped, and so the Jimmy Joyce Singers provided a new backing for the song — a heavenly chorus humming what sounded like "Battle Hymn of the Republic," and a few gospel-type "Amens" just before the verse about Martin Luther King.

The intention was to drive the song's emotional point home, in a way only television could do. In the process, John Abbott's soft arrangement was jettisoned - so much for the subtlety that Gernhard had so meticulously worked into the record.

The era of the single record's dominance was almost over — the album was taking over in a gradual shift that had begun with the Beach Boys' *Pet Sounds*, the Beatles' *Sgt. Pepper* and increased with the arrival of Hendrix, Cream, Joplin and their ilk.

So there would need to be a Dion album, featuring "Abraham, Martin and John." At Gernhard's suggestion, DiMucci drew up a list of the covers and original tunes he'd been performing in the Miami area. He sang each one into a cassette recorder, and sent the tapes to Gernhard in St. Petersburg. The recordings were forwarded to John Abbott in New York, who wrote lead sheets for the chosen songs.

The *Dion* album took two or three days to record at Allegro. Along with the hit single, it included "Everybody's Talkin'" and "The Dolphins" by Fred Neil, Joni Mitchell's "Both Sides Now" (still unknowns, Mitchell and Neil were frequent performers in the same Miami-area folk clubs as Dion), Bob Dylan's "Tomorrow is a Long Time," Leonard Cohen's "Sisters of Mercy" and Dion's peculiar but eerily evocative acoustic adaptation of "Purple Haze" by Jimi Hendrix.

Gernhard wrote the album's liner notes:

During the past five years, DION went from the top to obscurity. However, in the process he has become seasoned by this experience. The result is the birth of an extraordinary artist. His singing now expresses his personal world ...

... Working with DION has become a very real personal experience for me, because Laurie and DION together have created a LP that we hope will provoke you as it does me to thinking about all those things that in our day to day existence we continue to push in the background. When you listen to this album, we hope it gives you a good kick in the gut.

His comeback secure, Dion's first move was to bite the hand that had helped him. He left Laurie Records for a big-royalty deal with Warner Brothers. Between 1970 and '72, he would cut three acoustic albums for the label — *Sit Down Old Friend, You're Not Alone* and *Sanctuary*, all of them produced by Phil Gernhard. They all flopped. He and Gernhard never quite bonded as friends, either, and when the contract expired, so did their tenuous relationship.

8

Someday Soon

"He could hand out the candy when he wanted something. And he had everybody's attention. But when it got down to the cuttin,' well, if you were in the way, too bad. Phil was a 'Me, Me, I' guy — if it didn't do him any good, he just wasn't interested."

Barry Winslow

Because he spent more time with Gernhard than anyone, even Sandy, Ronny Elliott got to know a darker side of the Man With the Golden Ear. For all his earnestness and enthusiasm, Gernhard was stubborn to a fault.

"It was more than that he was full of himself," Elliott said. "He knew he was a hotshot. He had a real opinion of his ears, and that kind of thing, but it wasn't that he thought he was better than anybody ... he was an odd one all the way around."

For a man in the "youth" business, Gernhard was — like his father - proudly conservative. "When the money was really starting to come in, because of 'Snoopy,' he bought a new Toronado. That was a lot of money. There was a bumper sticker on it: 'We're in. Let's win.' Meaning Vietnam. So he wasn't your everyday hippie."

In due course, the Toronado was replaced by a gaudy blue Cadillac.

To his clients, to the suits at the record companies, to the press and to the public, Gernhard oozed confidence. Privately, it was another matter. "He could be a reasonably charming guy," Elliott remembered. "He just

Royal Guardsmen '69, From left, Richards, Taylor, Nunley, Balough and Winslow. Laurie Records publicity photo.

usually chose not to be."

Maurice Williams started calling from South Carolina. According to Elliott, "Phil would never take any of his calls. He really was not a believer in comebacks or second chances. To him, that was money that he'd made — and he had no interest in talking to Maurice at all. I don't know if he ever took any of his calls."

He could also be incredibly short-sighted. "I took him the Outlaws," said Elliott. "He passed on the band. That was very frustrating. Dick and Phil and I took the Outlaws to Miami, because Phil had never recorded at Criteria Studios. We worked for one day; we just did stuff all day long. We were thrilled, they were thrilled, everybody was happy.

"Phil and Dick and I went to dinner that night, and Phil said 'I've decided I'm not gonna do anything with this stuff. I'm not going to shop any of the material.' I said 'Why?' And he said 'Well, no one song jumps out at me.'

"One song was called 'Cookie Man,' and I don't remember the others, but they were all great. I said 'Look, why don't I pay for the sessions, and I shop this stuff?' And he said 'It's my stuff. It's not for sale.' That was the end of it. That's the way he was."

By the mid 1970s, the Tampa-based Outlaws — working with another producer - would go on to become one of the top-selling Southern Rock bands of all time, with a saddlebag full of hits like "There Goes Another Love Song," "Green Grass and High Tides" and "Hurry Sundown."

American music and its attendant culture was changing at an un-clockable clip in 1969. The clean-cut teen combos of the mid '60s had morphed into shaggy-haired "rock bands," playing longer and louder songs with more expressive lyrics and a new attenuation to the "freedom of expression" movement that was sweeping the nation's young people into uncharted new areas.

The Outsiders, who'd become the Soul Trippers, now became Noah's Ark. The Bay Area's "heavy bands" had names like Bethlehem Asylum, Split Ends, GAP and BOOT. They didn't play the Inn Crowd or the Spot or the Surfers Club — the hippest club around was now the psychedelical-ly-painted Electric Zoo.

In the midst of such tectonic plate-shifting, Gernhard got Holler a one-off deal with Laurie for a bizarre novelty number. "Amos-Ben-Haren-Hab-Seti-14," was a comedy song about an ancient Egyptian romance gone sour. It adhered closely to the wacky, poly-syllabic template created by funnyman Ray Stevens, whose "Gitarzan" was in the Top Ten the month Holler's single was released.

The Royal Guardsmen, meanwhile, were still under contract with Gernhard and pleading with him to unharness them from the novelty yoke. They weren't the same malleable schoolboys he'd signed to deliver his Snoopy song to the world.

Individualism was the order of the day. They too had grown their hair long, and dressed in jeans and flowing hippie gear. Most significantly, after three years of nearly constant gigging, the Guardsmen had matured and coalesced into a tight band.

They flew to New York with Gernhard and cut three songs: A new, "socially conscious" song of Holler's called "Mother, Where's Your Daughter," a cover of the venerable Rolling Stones ballad "As Tears Go By," and a screaming psychedelic freakout, credited to all six band members, titled "Magic Window."

Taylor, who'd originated the latter melody during soundchecks while the band was touring, played a thunderous church organ — a nod to his hero of the moment, Procol Harum's Gary Brooker. Richards howled like Clapton on guitar, and both Winslow and Nunley had adopted rock's new full-throated, bare-chested singing style.

"Mother, Where's Your Daughter/Magic Window" was issued by Laurie in the spring, immediately after Dick Holler's comedy record and a boiling, three-minute stoner rant ("Sheriff") by the Sarasota-area trio GAP. The Royal Guardsmen single was the only one of the three to stand a chance, commercially.

Ah, but it was a classic case of too little, too late. "He was just throwing us a bone," Taylor believed. "We had bitched so much about it — and he knew we could do so much better than that Snoopy stuff. He knew we were capable of that.

"We ate it up ... but we didn't even know 'Mother, Where's Your Daughter' had been released as a single."

It was, although it never got with spitting distance of the charts.

"We were pissed off at Gernhard and the record company. They wouldn't do anything. Gernhard just kept saying 'My hands are tied.' They were tied from counting all that money!

"We could do stuff like 'Mother, Where's Your Daughter' and 'I Say Love' and 'So Right' and 'As Tears Go By,' we could do way better things than that, and they just wouldn't let us do it."

Under pressure from his parents to return to college full-time, and weary of the grind anyway, Billy Taylor quit the Royal Guardsmen. Similarly burned out, Barry Winslow bailed too, encouraged by Gernhard's vague promises of a solo career. After a string of summer tour dates, including two nights at Madison Square Garden in June, opening for Canada's Guess Who, Richards and Burdett walked away. Nunley and Balogh limped along for a while, using replacement members.

But it was all over.

To paraphrase Rodney Dangerfield, when the Royal Guardsmen broke up, the Royal Guardsmen were the only ones who knew they'd broken up.

Gernhard, however, had one more trick up his sleeve — and he didn't need the band to help him pull it off.

In the summer of 1969, America was in the grip of lunar fever. NASA had sent its Apollo astronauts to orbit the moon, and the big moment

— when Neil Armstrong and Buzz Aldrin would walk on the lunar surface — was scheduled for July.

It was to be another watershed moment in the country's history, and Gernhard sensed fresh opportunity. He and Holler dug Snoopy and the German out of the closet, dusted them off and wrote another song, with yet another variation of the melody and the old Johnny Horton march tempo.

They called it "The Smallest Astronaut (A Race to the Moon With the Red Baron)," and booked time to record it, using Barry Winslow and the same gang of studio musicians, at Allegro.

But Schulz, no doubt as weary of the whole franchise as the public, refused to let them use his dynamic dog in another of their songs.

"We told him hey, this could be good for everyone," Holler recalled, "but Schulz said no, he's already been to the moon. One of the astronauts brought a Snoopy doll on a flight around the moon, and Snoopy had on a toy astronaut suit.

"We said, 'But he only flew around it!' Nope. End of Schulz association." Poof.

The lyrics were hastily re-written, and "The Smallest Astronaut" was recorded in the same basic style as the "Snoopy" hits, with no mention of the beagle at all. Released in July, in time for the historic moon landing, it was credited to Barry Winslow, not the Royal Guardsmen. "We were hoping that the Royal Guardsmen fans, and the Snoopy fans, would recognize the sound and the same lead vocalist," Holler said. "But it didn't fly."

Elliott, meanwhile, knew how to push Gernhard's buttons. "Phil said, 'Hey Ronny, don't you want to get in on the pool?' Everybody kicks in $10 and guesses how many units their new release would sell in its first week.

"Laurie was just releasing 'The Smallest Astronaut.' I guessed 200; Phil said "200,000?" And I said "No, 200 units." He still took my money, but that made him so mad! And I won the pool."

Gernhard Enterprises was still producing concerts. "I did more than Phil did when it came to actually doing the shows, but Phil was obsessive about the radio promotion," Elliott said. "It was our biggest expense, number one. He would sit for hours with the sales people from WFSO and WLCY, buying spots — and then they meet for a couple hours changing it around. Last-minute things if it looked like we weren't going to do well."

His behavior could be erratic and impossible to predict, Elliott explained. "He'd say 'I think we're going to do well tomorrow night — if we do, there's a big bonus for you.' Then we would sell out. OK, we couldn't do better. And he would never mention any bonus.

"We would lose $10,000 in a night — it wasn't my money, but it would just kill me. In some ways, it's harder to lose other people's money than it is your own. And then out of the clear blue, he would write me a $3,000 check and slide it across the desk. So none of it ever made sense. None of it ever made business sense. Why did he do it? I don't know."

Gernhard the entrepreneur cast his eye towards more civic matters in the fall of '69 by negotiating with the City of St. Petersburg Beach for a retail concession building on Pass-a-Grille, a spit of public beach popular with locals and tourists. The lot in question — a half-mile south of the legendary Don CeSar Hotel, one of St. Petersburg's few actual landmarks - had been the site of the historic Pass-a-Grille Hotel, which had burned to the ground two years before, leaving a massive concrete slab as the only evidence it existed. Now the city was trying to figure out what to do with the parcel, which was strategically located right on the beach sand. It was a primo spot, and Gernhard wanted it.

A group of citizens took the city to court, arguing that the old hotel site had been part of the public beach, and as such was not city-owned, and not available to the highest bidder. "We already have enough beer places on the beach," resident Ben Rugglero argued.

At one particularly contentious meeting, comments by Stanley E. Butler, treasurer of the Pass-a-Grille Community Association, were followed by cheers and applause that drowned out the commissioners' gavels.

"Pass-a-Grille is disgusted with the drunkenness and rowdyism associated with the many booze joints near the former beach hotel site," Butler crowed. "Most residents of Pass-a-Grille want a clean, green park, where they can sit and enjoy the beauty, particularly the gorgeous sunsets.

"I want to put down this idea once and for all," Gernhard said. "What we want to build will be beautiful, particularly the landscaping. And it will be a whole lot better than having the kids run across a busy street and go into a bar and buy soft drinks.

"Sure we want to sell beer. People like it. But our lease would not permit a juke box there, or anything conducive to loitering, and we must close at sundown."

He told the assembled that Walt Disney World, when it opened in a year or so, was going to change tourism everywhere, including St. Petersburg Beach.

"It may surprise you, Phil," countered Stanley Butler, "that the overwhelming majority of our residents don't want a flood of people here from Disney World, and consider it somewhat of an intrusion rather than a business opportunity."

Kent LaVoie, the singer and guitar player for the Sugar Beats, had been pitching songs to Gernhard Enterprises since the office opened in '67, hoping to get something recorded. Phil wasn't a big fan of the young Floridian's quiet, breathy singing voice. "You'll never get a deal as a singer," he told LaVoie. "If you want to get anything this business, you gotta write it."

Challenge accepted. "That was all he needed to say to me," LaVoie explained. "For the next three years, if his car was there, I was there.

"I followed along behind him, like a little doggie. Because I had to do what he wanted, and what he wanted was songs. And I wrote, and I wrote. He wouldn't be there 10 minutes and I was there. If he wasn't there, if he was gone to California or something, it would kill my day. Horrible."

Gernhard rejected one song after another, but LaVoie was undeterred. Finally, in the summer of '69, he came into the office with something Gernhard could not ignore: A sweet, country-flavored pop song about the New York Mets, who were having an unprecedented season after a lengthy losing streak. The team's spring training camp was in St. Petersburg, just a few blocks from the Gernhard offices (and not far from LaVoie's house), and so the city caught a serious case of baseball fever as the underdog team battled its way toward the World Series.

"I used to call myself a mercenary songwriter," LaVoie reflected. "Because Phil was hammering into me at the time, AM radio hits. Had nothing to do with making albums, had nothing to do with the meaning of the songs or anything.

"I was just trying to write a hit about anything. It made absolutely no difference to me — I wasn't trying to prove anything except, write a hit. And especially in St. Petersburg, this thing with the Mets was a big deal. Everybody was caught up in it, if you were a sports fan at all."

He took "Happy Days in New York City" to Gernhard. "And then I found out what it's like to have somebody excited over a song. Two weeks later, I was in New York playing with the top musicians at the time. With the string section playing live. It was just the most wonderful thing I had ever done when they overdubbed the strings on that. And I'm sitting there listening to it and about crying, you know? This is the Big Time."

With a few lyrical tweaks by Gernhard, "Happy Days in New York City" was recorded at Allegro, with an arrangement by John Abbott and crystalline background harmonies from members of the Left Banke.

LaVoie's single, the last Gernhard would ever make for Laurie, dropped just as the Mets were clinching the Series in October.

"All the Mets had to do was win the Series and I was going to have a smash," LaVoie said. "Then they won, and that was the end of that! It was never heard by anybody."

"Happy Days in New York City" didn't catch on, but it hatched a professional relationship that would take them both to bigger and better places — places Gernhard had only dreamed about - in the dawning decade.

In January 1970, Gernhard told the *Evening Independent* that his company was getting out of the concert promotion business (Sandy, who found the whole rock promotion thing distasteful and full of sleazy people, was thrilled).

Gernhard Enterprises' last concert, he said, would be the Feb. 20 Rock & Roll Revival Show at Curtis Hixon Hall. The oldies-but-goldies bill was to include Chuck Berry, Bo Diddley, Bill Haley and His Comets, Gene Vincent and the Coasters.

Duckbutter, Ronny Elliott's newest band, was in the opening slot.

"After that," Gernhard said with that exaggerated importance he often used when talking with reporters, "we're suspending any promotional activities, because in the last two weeks we've landed five major record contracts, and that's more than enough."

Along with his deal to produce Dion albums for Warner Brothers, he was to record a single for that label with a band from Birmingham, Alabama called Chair.

For MGM, he would record former Royal Guardsman vocalist Barry Winslow, and for Bell Records, Columbia Pictures' newly-created music subsidiary, the Jacksonville-based M.O.U.S.E. would cut a pair of singles.

And because of the success of "Abraham, Martin and John," Atlantic Records had agreed to pony up for a full Dick Holler album.

He also spoke vaguely about a contract with a movie company called Afro Embassy Pictures. "We're hoping to go into motion picture production someday," Gernhard explained (the "royal we" had started to creep into his conversations around this time, too).

"We did what we wanted to (with concert promotions)," he said. "We wanted to create some different kinds of music in the area, and we believe we did."

Booking time at New York's Mirasound Studios, and back at Criteria in Miami, Gernhard assembled a small band of studio players for Holler's album, *Someday Soon.*

Of course, "Abraham, Martin and John" was included (in a respectful arrangement) among the album's 10 songs, as was "Mother, Where's Your Daughter," which had been the Royal Guardsman's final single the year before.

> On his first album for Atlantic Records he has turned his talents to a graphic illustration of many of the tragic failures of the American social system.
>
> Revolution is no longer a word from our past — it lives today — possible, some say probable in the 1970's. Voices are calling, peaceful change is still desirable — is anybody listening?
>
> **Liner notes, Someday Soon**

As it turned out, nobody was listening at all, and Dick Holler's name wasn't added to the list of history's great recording artists known and respected for their calls for social upheaval.

In February, the St. Petersburg Beach City Commission approved Gernhard Enterprises' request for conditional use of their Pass-a-Grille site

for food and beer sales. The usually lethargic Tuesday-night commission meeting turned into a near-riot, as those Pass-a-Grille residents who opposed the deal shouted over the mayor and the commissioners. Gernhard was not in attendance.

After investing $50,000 on construction of the Pass-a-Grille concession stand, he would manage it until 1973, when he finally left Florida for the music business fast lane in Los Angeles.

Sandy's nephew Ed Wright worked at the stand for four years. "I was about 14 when Phil gave me a ride home from the concession stand," Wright recalled, "and as he would pass hitchhikers on the road, he would roll down the window on his Cadillac and yell 'Get a job.' He was not a patient man with lazy people. I admired that.

"I remember when Hurricane Agnes appeared in the Gulf of Mexico in 1972, it was (only) a Cat 1 storm, but it surely did a lot of damage, particularly at Pass-A-Grille beach. Phil risked his life to save the concession stand during the night of the storm, which destroyed his prized Cadillac, but saved his business.

"Once every so often, he would say things to me ... one was if/when you become successful and/or wealthy, don't overwhelm folks with it. It offends people, and it makes you out to be a fool. He said 'People always admire hard work, not those who ask for a handout. Kids need to get off their lazy backsides and work for it.'"

In autumn 1970, Phil Gernhard booked what would be one of the Tampa Bay area's most historic concerts. Nobody knew it at the time.

"Phil called me at home one night," Elliott recalled, "and said 'What do you think about doing Eric Clapton?' I had pretty much lost my enthusiasm for all the things we'd done so badly on so many shows, but I said 'Yeah, that's great. Let's do it.'

"He said 'Well, there's a hitch. He's put together a new band that they're calling Derek & the Dominos — apparently he's Derek, but we can't use his name. The only way we can say Eric Clapton in radio spots, ads and billboards is to list him as a member of this band, Derek & the Dominos.

Everything has to be alphabetical. There can't be a picture of him, just the band.'"

The Dominos album, *Layla and Other Assorted Love Songs*, would arrive in November, but if the show (Curtis Hixon had an open date Dec. 1) was going to happen, it had to be booked immediately.

Gernhard booked the concert. "Nothing was on the radio yet," said Elliott. "What the hell are we gonna do? It was touchy." Initial ticket sales, not surprisingly, were sluggish. "Derek & the Dominos" didn't mean anything to most music fans.

Meanwhile, one of Ronny's musician buddies was Berry Oakley, bassist for the Florida-based Allman Brothers Band, who hadn't quite hit it big yet — at that moment in time, they were touring behind their second album, *Idlewild South*.

On the afternoon of Nov. 28, the Allman band played an outdoor show at Florida Presbyterian College in St. Petersburg. Elliott had heard that Duane Allman — the band's brilliant, incendiary slide guitarist — was featured on nearly every track of the soon-to-be-released Derek & the Dominos album, offering fiery counterpoint to Clapton's passionate leadwork. Clapton had seen Allman live in Miami, during a break in recording sessions, and, awed, invited him into the studio to play with the Dominos.

Elliott told Oakley that the Dominos' tour would be stopping there in a few days. Oakley, in turn, told Allman, who made plans to stay in the Tampa Bay area for a while, as the Allman Brothers Band's tour was taking a break until Dec. 4.

"I didn't see Berry or any of the band after that, but the next week, when Derek & the Dominos came strolling in, there was Duane with Eric," Elliott said.

"In the meantime, we had a terrible scene. Some little jackass with an attache case and a British accent came in yelling and screaming, and flailing his arms about, saying 'That's it! Nobody's playing! We're going home!'"

In an attempt to be helpful, the Curtis Hixon staff — well aware of the show's pokey ticket sales, and unbeknownst by Gernhard or Elliott — had changed the marquee out front to read ERIC CLAPTON.

The little man, who was obviously someone important, was hysterical and ready to pull the plug. "After a lot of arguing and begging and

pleading, he said all right, OK, and the show went on."

Gernhard was nowhere to be found during all the afternoon drama. He did, however, make it to Curtis Hixon that night to witness the first of only two concerts that Duane Allman would play as a member of Derek & the Dominos (he jumped on the band bus and went onstage with Clapton and company in Syracuse the following night), before re-joining the Allman Brothers Band in Columbia, South Carolina.

In less than a month, Derek & the Dominos would cease to exist. In less than a year, Duane Allman would be dead (Clapton described him as "the musical brother I'd never had but wished I did").

Layla and Other Assorted Love Songs was an unmitigated flop upon its release, but over time came to be considered the high water mark of Clapton's recorded output. A lot of the credit was due Duane Allman, who, critics believed, drove and challenged the British guitar god to new heights of greatness.

Of the two Dominos shows that included Allman, only Tampa was recorded — albeit by an audience member on a hissy cassette tape. Still, because of its historical relevance, it is one of the most cherished bootleg recordings in existence.

The official Lobo look for '72, the era of his biggest hit "I'd Love You to Want Me." Big Tree Records publicity photo.

9

Introducing Lobo

INTRODUCING LOBO. Big Tree's first million seller, Lobo's "Me and You and a Dog Named Boo," made Top Five on the Hot 100 and No. 1 on the Easy Listening Chart. The group's first LP extends the gentle rock sound, with such memorable cuts as "We'll Make it - I Know We Will," "A Little Different," "Reaching Out for Someone," "She Didn't Do Magic" as well as the song that started it all.

Billboard
Album Reviews
June 5, 1971

As head of A&R for Laurie in the mid 1960s, Doug Morris helped nurse the struggling label back into the pink of its glory days. Not only had he worked closely with Gernhard on the Royal Guardsmen records and on Dion's "Abraham, Martin and John," he'd bought the master recording of a song called "Little Bit O' Soul," by Ohio's Music Explosion, and watched it sail up the charts to lodge in the No. 2 spot.

It spent two weeks there, unable to upset "Windy" by the Association, but it was nevertheless a bona fide smash.

Morris left the Schwartz Brothers' employ in 1970 and started an independent label called Big Tree Records. A distribution deal was struck with Ampex, the reel-to-reel tape manufacturer and a pioneer in the development of the pre-recorded cassette tape.

Phil Gernhard, his man in Florida, was one of the first independent producers Morris called. "Got anything for me?" Morris asked.

As a matter of fact, he did. Unphased by the failure of "Happy Days in New York City," Gernhard had continued to press his latest protégé, former Sugar Beat Kent LaVoie, for songs.

Nineteen-seventy was the year of the sensitive singer/songwriter, the hip, long-haired, heart-on-the sleeve troubadour. With James Taylor as the flagship artist, a movement had begun, and labels were rushed and panicked to find the next big soul-baring — and therefore money-generating - acoustic artist.

Gernhard, of course, had aided ex-teen heartthrob Dion in his quest for acceptance as an acoustic singer/songwriter, and had just started producing his album projects for Warner Brothers, James Taylor's label.

As an independent, however, Gernhard was not contractually bound to Warner or any other record company. He was free to work with whoever, whenever, wherever, as long as they wanted him.

And he and Dion hadn't developed much of a relationship outside of the studio.

Kent LaVoie had just presented Gernhard with a gently-strummed paean to the simple life called "Me and You and a Dog Named Boo."

"Phil thought Kent had hit records in him," said Ronny Elliott, who was still hanging around the office, despite the dramatic reduction in Gernhard Enterprises concerts for him to work on. "And I did, too. When Kent brought 'Me and You and a Dog Named Boo' into the office, Phil and I looked at each other, I didn't say anything because he wasn't saying anything. When Kent left, Phil said 'That's a big hit,' and I agreed. He said 'I don't want to waste it on Kent, though. I want you guys to do it.'"

"You guys" in this case was Duckbutter, Elliott's latest band. Playing a rocked-up blend of country, gospel and blues, the group was a showcase for vocal harmony — which was all the rage, because of the success of Crosby, Stills, Nash and company — and, of all things, redneck jokes and slapstick comedy. Even in those times of independence and individuality, Duckbutter's music was an unusual amalgam of styles.

Elliott: "A Duckbutter show had comedy, magic, drama and rocked and rolled like nothing else. It was dumb and it was sweet."

Elliott and his band took "Me and You and a Dog Named Boo" into the Charles Fuller studio to make a demo. "What I brought him back was all bottleneck guitar," according to Elliott. "Turned it into something I would love today! But it was no longer a hit record. I could tell that."

Gernhard nevertheless flew Duckbutter to New York, ostensibly to showcase the band for record labels. Also on the flight out of Tampa International were Kent LaVoie and his acoustic guitar. And "Me and You and a Dog Named Boo."

LaVoie played a handful of songs for Doug Morris, and subsequently became the first artist signed to Big Tree Records. "By that time," said Elliott, "Phil knew he was not gonna record it with us."

Released in the early days of 1971 as Big Tree 112, "Me and You and a Dog Named Boo" was not credited to Kent LaVoie. Instead the artist on the single was listed as a single word: Lobo.

"We used my real name on 'Happy Days in New York City' and it didn't do anything," LaVoie said. The decision was made to start all over, using a pseudonym.

"Phil said well, think of some names. So I made a list. I'm reading 'em, and I said 'Lobo.' He asked what it meant, and I said 'It's Spanish for wolf.' And he said 'That's it.' Just like that."

"Me and You and a Dog Named Boo" reached No. 5 in April 1971. "Phil came into the studio and said 'Me and You and a Dog Named Boo' did 67,000 performances the first quarter," LaVoie said. "You might as well have said to me 'I'm going to Czechoslovakia on a bus,' cause I didn't know what it meant."

When a song was played on the radio, and reported to the industry trade papers, that was a "performance." In today's money, LaVoie said, "that translates to about $500,000."

LaVoie was in St. Petersburg, driving at night to visit his wife at her place of employment, the first time he heard his little song over the airwaves. It was on the Chicago AM station WLS — the same station that had debuted "Snoopy vs. the Red Baron" all those years ago — and the signal, as usual, was dicey.

"WLS was fading in and out," he said. "It faded back in, and there was 'Me and You and a Dog Named Boo.' It was the strangest thing. It was an affirmation. It had nothing to do with money. It had nothing to do with being a star. I was pleasing Phil."

They were a team, Gernhard and LaVoie. "Phil called and said 'It's a smash.' And my heart fell in my foot. I said 'What do you mean?'

"He said 'We got an order for records out of Chicago.' Now, Phil was the one who'd had 500 Sugar Beats records pressed that he was selling out of his trunk. That's what a record deal was to me. So I asked him, 'how many records.' And he says 'The first order was 20,000.'"

Doug Morris was over the moon. Lobo, Big Tree's first artist, was already making money.

An album, *Introducing Lobo,* was hastily recorded. Because LaVoie didn't have enough songs to fill it out, Gernhard had him cut three from the Dick Holler catalog.

What LaVoie didn't realize was that Gernhard had backroom-brokered a deal giving himself majority ownership of LaVoie's songs.

"He had a piece of the publishing, which I didn't know till later," LaVoie said. "Doug Morris had a piece of it. Big Tree had a piece of it. I did all of the writing, and I had none of the publishing."

What did Kent LaVoie, 26 years old and selling millions of records, know about publishing deals? "As Roger Miller famously said, 'I got the first check that had a comma in it.' And when a quarter of it is equal the yearly salary you were making playing six nights a week, it changes your life."

Before the publishing arrangement was modified, in time, he only made money from record sales.

According to LaVoie, he'd learned how to deal with Gernhard. "I read Phil correctly, from early on, and that's the reason I was one of the few successes from Tampa. I read him that he had to be in control. You had to do it the way he wanted it done. If you crossed him, you were dead. There was no forgiveness. None."

Introducing Lobo — which didn't have a single photo of Kent LaVoie on the front or back covers - barely broke the Top 200 that summer, but work was already underway on a second album, to be called *Close Up.*

Ampex, meanwhile, was hemorrhaging money and getting out of the record business, and Morris had negotiated a distribution deal with Bell Records to take effect in 1972. "Phil didn't want me to write any songs for the album, because he knew they were going to bury it," LaVoie said.

"Phil made a deal. All he said was 'We're changing distributors, you need to sign,' so I did. I'm not stupid, but I knew where I was compared to where I started."

All the recording costs for *Close Up* — which would never be released - came out of LaVoie's advances.

Although he made money from live performances, Lobo toured infrequently. In fact, he rarely did interviews, enjoying the anonymity that came with hiding behind a stage name. He and Kathy remained in St. Petersburg; Mrs. LaVoie became close friends with Sandy Gernhard. "If 'Me and You and a Dog Named Boo' was the only hit, I could have lived off it my whole life, the way I live," he said.

Flush with Lobo cash, Gernhard flew the members of Duckbutter to New York to record one-off single he'd brokered with Paramount Records, the newly-minted music division of Paramount Pictures. He loved the demo Ronny Elliott had played him of a contagious, good-timey original song they called "Gospel Trip (Medley)."

Before that, according to Elliott, "Everything to him was too country. 'Peaceful Easy Feeling' by the Eagles came out and I thought 'Well, OK, I've won this argument.' I went to Phil and said 'Look at this.' He said 'OK, and I'll tell you what: It's a regional hit. Let's talk about this six months from now.'"

Gernhard was chastised — although he would certainly never admit it — and when Ronny and the boys came up with "Gospel Trip," he thought he might just have his own Eagles.

"He thought that Duckbutter should be the biggest thing in show business," Elliott said. "So he didn't want to put out something that would be JUST a hit record. He wanted us to be the Beatles."

"Gospel Trip," as the title suggested, was a medley of three separate songs, all of them tied to the then-current "Jesus Rock" trend. Norman Greenbaum's "Spirit in the Sky" had recently been a Top Five smash, and the straight-gospel Edwin Hawkins Singers won a Grammy for their record "Oh Happy Day."

So off they went, full of high hopes and adrenaline, to cut their single at Electric Lady, the very same studio where "Me and You and a Dog Named Boo" had been committed to tape.

"And when we walked out of there, he turned to me and said 'Your demo's better.' I said 'Yeah, I know.'

"So Duckbutter fell apart, and that was basically the end of my real relationship with Phil. I wasn't mad at him, but I was disappointed. Again."

The *actual* second Lobo album, *Of a Simple Man*, appeared late the next summer. This one included what would be LaVoie's biggest career hit, "I'd Love You to Want Me." Although it stalled at No. 2 in the States (behind "I Can See Clearly Now" by Johnny Nash), "I'd Love You to Want Me" went all the way in Germany (13 weeks at the top) and Australia (two weeks).

"It was Number One in *Cash Box* and *Record World*, but not in *Billboard*, thanks to Johnny Nash," LaVoie laughed.

LaVoie hired a California-based manager (Ruth Aarons, who also handled David Cassidy) and threw himself into public appearances. He was developing professional muscles.

He also began to examine more closely his contracts with Gernhard. "What Phil got for me was $275,000 up front, plus $175,000 for each of four albums," LaVoie said. "They cost about thirty to make in those days. So add it up, it's over a half-million dollars. Of which he was assured to have $125,000 in costs after that.

"Zero for me. That's when the hammer fell."

The friendship began to teeter on its heels. "If he had given me $50,000 out of the $175,000, and advanced me $25,000 an album, he would have been making a hundred thousand, or two hundred and I wouldn't have questioned it. It was more like me saying 'Hey, I helped! Throw some this way.' No way."

Gernhard was spending increasing amounts of time making deals and signing contacts in Los Angeles, where the music industry was based. It was around 1972 that he was introduced to Mike Curb, the boyish young president of MGM Records.

The California native had been writing songs, playing piano and producing records since the early '60s. "I was the first artist signed to the label after Warner/Reprise merged in 1964," Curb said.

"And I was their first artist that they didn't pick up the option on, too. (Label head) Mo Ostin said to me 'I think you might be better off just being a producer.' I guess that was a nice way of saying 'You're not an artist.' Anyway, I listened to him."

Curb and MGM were hot stuff in '72, with smash hits from the likes of the Osmonds and Sammy Davis Jr. (Davis' Grammy-winning recording of "The Candy Man," produced by Curb, prominently featured backing vocals by a clean-cut, multi-generational, all-American apple-pie singing group called the Mike Curb Congregation).

Curb and Gernhard spoke briefly at an industry event. "Phil, if you ever have a hit that you don't have a home for, let me know," Curb told the newly-famous Floridian.

Lobo hit the Top Ten for the third time in January of '73 with "Don't Expect Me to Be Your Friend," from *Of a Simple Man*.

LaVoie and Gernhard spent several months in Atlanta, recording the next Lobo album, *Calumet*, at Mastersound Studios.

Ex-Royal Guardsman Barry Winslow was struggling financially, so Gernhard hired him to run sound for a Lobo tour. Gernhard still thought he could break the Million Dollar Kid into the mainstream, so he convinced Big Tree to bankroll a test single.

He and LaVoie took the "Snoopy" singer into Mastersound and produced a Lobo-esque ballad, "Get to Know Me." Even though Winslow wrote the song, the publishing was split 50/50 between LaVoie and Gernhard. "Get to Know Me" was one more hit-that-should-have-been.

Another flop. Nobody made a dime.

LaVoie remembers the day he received a phone call, out of the blue, from a guitar player he knew in his Winter Haven teen days. Jim Stafford had even been in a band with him, the Legends (the group also briefly included future real-life legend Gram Parsons).

Since the success of Lobo, Kent LaVoie had become Winter Haven's only "hometown celebrity."

Stafford's solo act — just him and his guitar - was a hit in Gulfside beach bars and seafood restaurants. He'd self-recorded a live album at the Elbow Room, a touristy supper club in a swanky Sarasota suburb called St. Armand's Key, and sold it out of the trunk of his car.

"I happened to be in Clearwater doing a photo session, and he was playing on the beach," LaVoie remembered. "He found my number and called to see if I'd come out to hear his songs; he wanted me to record them."

LaVoie really, *really* didn't feel like it. But he was intrigued. And he hadn't spoken with Stafford in years.

Stafford was booked at the Shack Upon the Beach, a combination motel, bar and restaurant.

"We were drinking beer," recalled LaVoie, and I'm thinking 'I told him I'd come; I'm gonna hear this shit and get out of here and I'll be through with it.'

"He turns the tape on and it goes *Blackwater Hattie lived back in the swamp where the strange green reptiles crawl. Snakes hang thick from cypress trees, like sausage from a smokehouse wall ...*"

Gulp. LaVoie had not expected anything so weird, and yet so damn cool. "I said 'You got anything else?'"

The song was a talking blues provisionally titled "Blackwater Hattie," what the composer called "a poem set to music." Layered with acoustic slide guitars, it was eerie and atmospheric, almost Southern gothic in flavor.

He didn't care for any of Stafford's other songs, like "I Ain't Sharin' Sharon" or "Nifty Fifties Blues," and eventually the conversation returned to "Blackwater Hattie." A Lobo record, with that haunted-house vocal? Probably not.

LaVoie: "He said 'Yeah, that's the one I thought you could do.' I said 'Jim, you're the artist. I couldn't do this song. You need to record this yourself.'"

And then he had an epiphany: I'll get Phil in on this.

The next night, he brought Gernhard, and together they caught Stafford's performance — equal parts music and comedy - in front of an audience. "It was in this little bitty club, just him and a guitar," LaVoie explains. "Now, growing up, all he did was play Chet Atkins guitar. I didn't know he told jokes. It was the way he said it — the delivery! I couldn't believe that was him."

At 29, Stafford had been kicking around clubs in Florida and Georgia for nearly a decade when he first crossed paths with Gernhard. "I worked at trying to figure out how to entertain people," Stafford said. "I worked hard on the guitar, and I had tried to figure out how to sing."

What he wanted to be was a showman, an all-around entertainer. The Victor Borge of the guitar.

Stafford was a guitarist of considerable prowess. He'd carved his niche — such as it was — by writing and singing funny, sometimes off-color or politically-incorrect songs in a goofy, good-ol-boy voice, punctuating them with serious hotshot guitar tunes like "Malaguena" and "Classical Gas." He also tore it up on the banjo. He was immensely likeable.

At Sarasota's Elbow Room and at a nightclub in Clearwater, the Glass Frog, he was a big draw. But he wanted more.

When Stafford played the little cassette demo of his bayou voodoo song, Gernhard was sold. Sure, he'd cut a handful of clunkers, but he trusted his ears — he knew a great song when he heard it, and he knew there and then that Jim Stafford was going to be a star.

"I think he saw potential in me not only as a singer/songwriter, but also as a person who could do a show," Stafford said. "And he plugged himself in from there on out."

Gernhard, LaVoie and Stafford came together at Mastersounds, the Atlanta studio where most of the Lobo work was done, for Stafford's first-ever recording session.

It was Gernhard who suggested they change the name of the song to "Swamp Witch," and LaVoie who requested he and Gernhard produce the spec single together, since LaVoie had "found" Stafford and brought him in.

Gernhard agreed, papers were signed, and yet another collaboration began.

Jim Stafford's first publicity shot, MGM Records, 1974. He would become Gernhard's latest golden goose.

10

You Fool, You Fool

The old spiders and snakes play is taking Jim Stafford's new single
SPIDERS AND SNAKES straight to the top of the charts. The single has
bullets and stars in all three trades this week. Watch for the album
being rush-released by MGM Records.

Billboard
MGM Records advertisement
Dec. 8, 1973

Mike Curb was Producer of the Year for 1972 in *Billboard*, and at the awards ceremony in Los Angeles he was approached again by Phil Gernhard. "Phil was one of the top ten producers that year as well," said Curb. "He said 'You know, I might take you up on bringing an act to you.' And he came back to me and played 'Swamp Witch' by Jim Stafford.

"It was incredible. It was like a Tony Joe White record. A very bayou-sounding record. Very Southern. We immediately made a deal, and we put out the single."

In July '73, "Swamp Witch" — on MGM Records - reached its peak chart position — a respectable 39 — in *Billboard*. "'Swamp Witch' sold half a million copies," Stafford recalled, "but it wasn't enough for me to get a lot of work. I wound up doing the state college circuit. Up in New York or New Jersey, we opened for this guy, and I couldn't figure out how somebody

I'd never heard of had roadies and a big band. I was just flabbergasted that a complete unknown would have the same stuff you have on the road when you're famous.

"The kid's name was Bruce Springsteen."

Stafford's "road crew" at the time consisted of his friend Leo Gallagher, a Tampa writer and comedian who held a degree in English Literature from the University of South Florida. Gallagher, as he would be known professionally, had done voiceover work for radio commercials and documentary films at Charles Fuller Productions.

For now, he was on the road with Jim Stafford, setting up his equipment, hanging out with his buddy and helping to write his stage routines.

From the start, it was clear to everyone Gallagher heard the beat of a different drummer (although he wouldn't start sledgehammering watermelons onstage for another couple of years).

"I wrote a novel called *The Mailman Cometh*," Gallagher said, "about the horn of plenty of sex in America, printed 5,000 copies on newsprint, loaded up my car and drove to every car race and rock concert on the Eastern Seaboard, selling them for what I could get. It was usually a dime. Sometimes a quarter.

"Sometimes I read to people. Sometimes I just got a beer and a sandwich. Eventually I came back home. My car was broke. I was broke."

They were back in Venice, south of Sarasota, playing another pay-the-rent club gig when fortune finally smiled on Jim Stafford.

Gernhard was flying back and forth between Florida and California, meeting with Curb and his executives, setting up TV appearances and making tour plans for Lobo ... and auditioning songs for Jim Stafford's album. "Swamp Witch" had been enough of a success that the label was asking for more.

"Phil showed up with a reel to reel recorder, and a tape of some of the things he had," Stafford said. "I showed him what I had. He played me the whole tape and then asked my opinion. And I told him that the song with the 'spiders and snakes' chorus had real potential. In my opinion.

"It was acoustic and a little bit like a Beatles song: ... *and that ain't what it takes to love me. Come on, love me!* I kept thinking of 'Love Me Do.' I took the thing over to my house in Winter Haven, and I worked on it. I worked a long time on it and every now and then, I'd go back in."

Growing up on a cattle ranch in a little town called Darby, north of St. Petersburg in rural Pasco County, Howard Bellamy and his younger brother David knew the value of hard work (their dad, Homer Bellamy, ran a tight ship) and the importance of playtime (Homer was also a part-time country and bluegrass musician who taught his guitar-strumming sons how to whoop it up for an audience).

The brothers formed a rock 'n' roll band called Jericho, and like so many hungry young Florida musicians they found their way north to Gainesville and the University of Florida, where fraternities always needed bands to entertain at their keg parties.

A cover band that also played some Bellamy originals, Jericho enjoyed a couple of good years on a frat-party circuit alongside Jacksonville's Lynyrd Skynyrd, and Gainesville's own Mudcrutch (which would morph, some years later, into Tom Petty & the Heartbreakers).

By 1973, the band was history, and the brothers were back tending cattle in Darby. David was turning out songs by the tractor-load and sending them out to producers, promoters, anyone who would listen; that's how "Spiders and Snakes" got to Phil Gernhard, and then to Jim Stafford.

Stafford turned what had been written as a straightforward, if a bit silly, rock 'n' roll song and turned it into broad comedy, to suit his style.

"'I don't like spiders and snakes, and that ain't what it takes to love me,' I wouldn't have touched that with a gun to my head," Stafford said. "I thought that was perfect. I wanted it to be sassier, so I added 'You fool, you fool.' Then sang it again and added 'Like I want to be loved by you.'"

Stafford committed his version to cassette, and drove it from Venice up to the Gernhard Enterprises office in St. Petersburg.

"I walked in and gave Phil the tape," Stafford remembered. "He put it on, he played it, and all he said was 'I gotta get out of here.' So we drove around for a while and talked. I think that Phil knew that I had nailed that song, and he couldn't sit still. He had to leave the office.

"He was sure that he had something. And he was excited enough that he wanted to get out of there. I don't remember a lot of what we talked about, probably all kinds of stuff. He was probably thinking about planning trips, where he was gonna cut it and who he was gonna use."

"Spiders and Snakes" became the first recording Gernhard made in Los Angeles (in this case, at the legendary Wally Heider Studios). As per

Howard, left, and David Bellamy, straight off the Pasco County ranch. Warner/Curb Records publicity photo.

their arrangement, Lobo would be credited as co-producer on the single. LaVoie had great ideas in the studio, said Stafford, and even sang high background vocals in places to create an octave-apart unison sound. A female singer was hired to provide the desired "sassy" vocalizations on the chorus.

The writing credit was changed from "David Bellamy" to "Jim Stafford and David Bellamy." And Gernhard, through his company Kaiser Music (named after Sandy's Siamese cat), assigned himself a share of the publishing. Kent LaVoie also got a cut.

David Bellamy was 22 years old with stars in his eyes, and oh, so ready to shake the Darby dust off his boots. "When I got to Gernhard's office he didn't say a word about cutting 'Spiders and Snakes,' though I found out later that he had already recorded it," Bellamy later wrote in *Let Your Love Flow*, the Bellamy Brothers' memoir. "At this meeting, he was all business. He bluntly told me that he had prepared the necessary contracts to get things rolling.

"That was an understatement. He'd prepared a songwriting contract, a publishing contract, an artist recording contract and a contract that made him my manager. Oh, and just in case that wasn't enough, the manager's contract also gave him power of attorney and the publishing contract assigned all my publishing rights to him."

Naturally, Bellamy signed the contract without batting an eye ("I'll be honest with you," he confesses in his autobiography. "I didn't even know what music publishing was.")

In the closing week of 1973, "Spiders & Snakes" got to No. 3 in the *Billboard* pop singles chart — a smash success for Stafford, LaVoie, Gernhard and Mike Curb's MGM.

The success of this single corresponded with the end of Phil's marriage to Sandy. He was spending more time in Los Angeles than in St. Petersburg, and was talking about closing Gernhard Enterprises for good and throwing in his lot with Mike Curb.

In California, he was turning into a big wheel. And he liked it.

New Jersey singer Tony Scotti, a square-jawed former University of Maryland football star, had large aspirations. He made a pair of flop singles for Liberty in the '60s, and also dabbled in acting (he played Sharon Tate's paramour, also called Tony, in *Valley of the Dolls*).

He'd been trying to crack the showbiz nut for a while. "As an actor, I might have to work for years and years and maybe won't get discovered until late in life," Scotti told writer Al Aronowitz in a *Saturday Evening Post* article called "The Dumb Sound" in 1963. "I want to be a film star, but I don't want to have to wait that long. My friends tell me I have a good voice, a good commercial sound. So that's what I'm going to do. I'm going to start cutting records. I'm going to sing my way into the movies."

After his "big break" in *Valley of the Dolls* came and went, the good-looking, smooth-talking sports hero gave it all up for a career in the business end of music. His older brother Ben, another ex-football star who'd played for the Washington Redskins and the Philadelphia Eagles, was working as a vice president of the promotions department at MGM Records; Tony sold himself as a producer and promoter, joined his brother, and in 1971 he was named a senior vice president, two years into Mike Curb's tenure as president. He worked in both A&R and promotions capacities.

Scotti expanded his role in the Curb family, as part of a "Sunshine Pop" harmony group called "Heaven Bound." With Joan Medora on lead vocals, and a Mike Curb Congregation-type backup chorus consisting of Scotti, Eddie Madora and Curb staff producers Tony Oliver and Michael Lloyd, a forgettable album — with Scotti credited as producer - was issued on MGM in 1972.

Scotti dated, and then married, Curb's sister Carole, making it a genuine family affair. "On their honeymoon, they went to see Jim Stafford," Mike Curb remembered with a chuckle, and that - presumably - was when Tony Scotti first met Phil Gernhard.

"I was transitioning out of MGM because Metro-Goldwyn Mayer wanted to sell the record company," Curb explained. "We had taken it over when it was losing a lot of money. It started making a profit with Donny Osmond, the Osmond Brothers, Sammy Davis Jr., Lou Rawls and the Sylvers.

"Tony was my brother-in-law, so I wanted him to have a nice transition, and obviously Phil, too ... I thought the relationship was a good one."

Although Gernhard-Scotti Enterprises wasn't registered as a corporation until July 1974, Gernhard and Scotti had decided to throw in together much earlier. Gernhard was starstruck, and he wanted to be a part of the big record-making machine in L.A. Nearly all of Gernhard-Scotti Productions' work would come under the Curb umbrella, as part of the label's newly-minted distribution deal with Warner Bros. Records.

They leased three small white bungalows at 9229 Sunset Boulevard, a hip neighborhood in the '70s, when appearances were crucial. Ben Scotti's promotion business — which would go on to work records at radio for the likes of ABBA and Barbra Streisand — was installed there, too.

With her husband gone so much of the time, splitting his efforts between Lobo and Stafford and now the Scottis, Sandy Gernhard — sitting at home in St. Petersburg - was questioning some of the choices she'd made.

When Phil swept her off her feet back in '63, she'd been cloistered, virginal Catholic schoolgirl eager to get away from an overbearing mother. She'd loved him then, not just for his brilliant mind and his handsome, all-American good looks, but for the way he included her in all of his activities, finding the artists, running the office and making the records. She'd thought of them as partners.

Ten years had gone by, and Sandy was a different woman. Just as Phil was a different man. She began to wonder what he was up to out there, if he was being faithful. If he was indulging in drugs and the other Bacchanalian trappings of the record business.

Phil's new business partners, so Sandy believed, saw her as the only impediment to his permanent relocation to La La Land. "The Scotti brothers hated me," she said. "They wanted him in California, but he didn't want to go ... I didn't want him to go."

But, of course, he went. "I feel guilty, because the friends that know me say I never should have divorced him. Because if he had that anchor here, it would have at least kept him a little distracted and he'd come home. In retrospect, he had to grow up, to go to California, cut his own records and do his own studio work. It got bad when he was out there."

Meaning the drinking, the drugs - and the shady business deals.

According to Sandy, Phil was truly crushed when she divorced him, instead of agreeing to the trial separation he'd proposed. "I had to break away. I had gone from being Mama's little girl to his little girl. I was the baby - this was the same thing, and I knew that."

Gernhard hired a lissome young brunette, Deborah Triplett, as his assistant. Triplett had escaped her one-horse North Carolina hometown to see the world as an airline stewardess, eventually settling in New York City. Triplett landed at job at 914 Studios, in Blauvelt, just outside the city, where Bruce Springsteen would record his first two albums.

When that relationship ended she went to Los Angeles, where she met a man and married him. Triplett was in the later stages of a nasty divorce when she started work at Gernhard-Scotti's offices on Sunset.

"I had a very physically and verbally abusive husband," she said. "At one point he actually knocked out my front teeth. He was calling the office and threatening everybody. He was a complete maniac. He knew no fear."

In 1973, Deborah Triplett and her first
husband appeared on the cover of
Playgirl *Magazine.*

Cue the white knight. "Phil Gernhard saved my life," Triplett explained. "It was really hard at the time to get any kind of protection. Phil got me a car, and paid for a bodyguard to be with me 24/7. He hadn't even known me that long! He said 'Deborah, I just knew somebody needed to help you, or you were gonna be dead.' He was such a good man."

She had a desk in Gernhard's bungalow, the first line of defense when visitors appeared; the Scottis worked together in the next one over. At the end of the strip was legendary Hollywood agent George "Bullets" Durgom, a 4-foot-9 fireball of Lebanese ancestry who'd started out as "band boy" for Glenn Miller and Tommy Dorsey in the '40s, the latter of which resulted in a lifelong friendship with Frank Sinatra.

For 11 years, Durgom managed Jackie Gleason. His other clients in the mid 1970s included Merv Griffin and the stage comic Mort Sahl. Durgom had just the sort of show business connections Gernhard understood were necessary to make a full-fledged star out of Jim Stafford. The energetic, affable agent told everybody that Stafford reminded him of "Gleason in his heyday."

Phil was starting to swim with big fish, and he was enjoying it. Suddenly there were gold rings on his fingers, and perpetual sunglasses, and expensive cigars in place of the plastic-tipped minis he's become addicted to in Florida. He mastered hip-speak and double-talk.

"He knew people," said LaVoie. "He had connections that were unbelievable. I don't know how he did it. He could pick up the phone and make things happen."

The Bellamys called him "Black Bart" behind his back, "For his shades, his dark clothes and the way he sulked around with a gold Quaalude on a chain around his neck, smoking his little spaghetti western cigar and scowling at everybody."

The boys from Pasco realized they weren't on the farm any longer.

"I did have one tough guy moment my first visit to Ben Scotti's office," David recalled. "Ben was on the phone when I walked in with his secretary. She told him who I was and he asked us to give him a minute. He went back to his phone conversation without missing a beat and said very matter-of-factly to the party on the other end of the line, 'If you don't play that record, I'm gonna break your fuckin' legs.' Then he politely hung up the phone and said 'Hey kid, nice to meet you. I was just promoting your song to the radio.'"

Gernhard leased a big house in Beverly Hills and developed a friendship with the actress Elke Sommer, who lived nearby.

Still, according to Stafford, "he never seemed to be happy with any women in his life that I know of. Phil was really not that interested in getting next to anybody. That would be my opinion. I don't think he was all that friendly. Kind of a strange guy. He drank an awful lot; he was a little bit self-destructive."

In the Hollywood Heights section of Los Angeles, on Cahuenga Drive within spitting distance of the Hollywood Bowl, Phil and Bullets set Stafford up in a two-story house of his own. "Jodie Foster lived down the street secretly," said Gallagher, who had the first floor to himself. "Across the street was a house built for Charlie Chaplin's girlfriend Pola Negre."

Stafford lived with Madeline Calder, a woman Gernhard had hired as an independent promoter in the early days of "Swamp Witch." A New Yorker who'd once worked for filmmaker Mel Brooks, Calder had joined Stafford, Gallagher and Gernhard in Dayton, Ohio, where William Morris agents had flown to catch Stafford's act.

The agents signed him, Calder and Stafford got involved, and everybody went west for what Calder would always remember as "The Hollywood Adventure."

She can still see Gernhard, smoking one of his pretentious little cigars, and pontificating as they all stood on a hotel balcony overlooking L.A. "One day," he said, gesturing, "all this is gonna be ours."

Gernhard then became romantically involved with Scottish singer Eve Graham, whose group the New Seekers had recorded for MGM. He and Scotti flew to London to meet with her and attempt to coax her into signing with them as a solo artist.

Graham signed, and before long she was living in Gernhard's house in Beverly Hills.

"Tony worked with me on my stage show, while Phil recorded me," Graham recalled. "I then had to kick my heels while they were setting up their record deal."

Several sides were recorded for Gernhard-Scotti Enterprises, with Phil — alone — at the console. "I never once saw Tony anywhere near a studio," Graham recalled, "even in the couple of years the New Seekers recorded at MGM, when he was vice president. Everybody in an American company is a vice president."

Graham described Gernhard in this period as "a loving, caring and

Tampa comedian Leo Gallagher lived with Jim Stafford, David Bellamy and Howard Bellamy in the Hollywood Hills. Atlantic Records publicity photo.

gentle man. And although I was happy living with him, he could become withdrawn. There were long hours in the studio, I sometimes got lonely, and eventually I went home to Scotland for Christmas, and stayed there."

They saw each other once, in Las Vegas after she re-joined the New Seekers. Gernhard was there with Stafford, who was performing at Harrah's. They had a long and friendly conversation.

"We spoke on the phone when he was in Nashville, and he said he was sorry, and that things would have been different had he not been an alcoholic. I confess I was so naive in 1974, I hadn't realized he had a drink problem."

Things were moving fast in the co-caine-and-champagne record business of the mid 1970s. Through Scotti's connections, Gernhard flew to London to record the British pop singer Petula Clark. She and Gernhard cut a single — it was the dawning days of sparkly, strobe-lit dance records, before the word "disco" had been formally introduced — and, wouldn't you know, it was a Dick Holler song, with an awkward, impossible-to-remember title: "Never Been a Horse That Couldn't Be Rode."

In all, Clark — a million miles from her "Downtown" heyday in the '60s - recorded four unremarkable songs with Gernhard, one of them a Kent LaVoie original called "Let's Sing a Love Song."

A veteran of musical theater, Clark liked to record as if she were on-stage — sing a song all the way through to the end, then do it all again if necessary. She was annoyed by Gernhard's patch-and-punch studio technique, crafting a tune sometimes one line at a time. They did not get along.

Deborah Triplett had been Gernhard's assistant for almost two years. "I started to fall in love with Phil because of that generosity of spirit that he had," she said. "Also, speaking as a female, I always found him very sexy. Because he was his own man. Phil owed nobody. Phil Gernhard made Phil Gernhard. And I never saw him kow-tow to anyone in the music business — or any business, for that matter."

And so Deborah moved in with him. "Phil always said I had great ears, too," she said. "So any time he had a song, he'd bring it home and play it, and he'd say 'Well, what do you think?' And then he'd go on and on about it."

They weren't terribly social, preferring to stay home most nights. "I was so gregarious and outgoing, I was his opposite," said Triplett. "I think that was part of his attraction to me. But on some levels we were very similar."

Phil's beverage of choice was Jack Daniels over shaved ice. "He would get drunk at home," she said, "but when he went to work he was very clear-headed." He and his crowd were also fond of Quaaludes, the unofficial drug of the decade.

By the end of '74 Stafford was an across-the-board smash. After "Swamp Witch" and "Spiders and Snakes" came more comedy hits, "My Girl Bill" and "Wildwood Weed." They all appeared on the MGM album *Jim Stafford*, rounded out with the rest of the tunes Stafford had played for LaVoie that afternoon at The Shack Upon the Beach in Clearwater. The songs LaVoie thought were lame. Gernhard put them on the album anyway.

"After 'Swamp Witch,' this is when Phil started pulling back from me," LaVoie remembers. "All of a sudden, Jim was more important than me. And all of a sudden it's really starting to piss me off."

He started looking more closely at the way Gernhard did business. "We got a checking account on Jim Stafford," LaVoie said. "Phil said 'You take care of it.' The checks came in, we signed them and I put them in the account. Which I thought was just eerie.

"The first check we got for Stafford was $101,000. Jim got I think $1,600. That's the way Phil Gernhard's record deals were. I got 50 or something like that, and Phil got 50. I did it, I put it in the bank, and I kept it, but I felt slimy."

With his already-severe distaste for the record business, the success of his old buddy Jim Stafford — and the way Gernhard was gleefully profiting from it — LaVoie began to get nervous. Following a late Lobo session at Mastersound, the Atlanta studio, the two repaired to the hotel bar. This was their usual routine while recording: After work, get positively legless before stumbling back to their respective rooms, sleep it off and do everything again the next day.

LaVoie began to seethe until he couldn't hold it in any longer. "I said 'Phil, listen. I'm probably not going to want to do this much longer, and I'd kind of like to have control of my own self. Why don't we just trade? I'll just take myself, and you can have Stafford?'

"I don't remember how the physical fight started, but all of a sudden we were down on the floor and I had him down by the neck, and I said 'You don't want to do this any more!' And he backed off. He was a chickenshit.'"

The fact that Gernhard had been making money from Lobo publishing — with LaVoie himself getting only record sale profits and money from live appearances — had been eating away at him. "When Phil and I finally worked out an agreement, when he finally had to pay the money he owed me and the split was this and the split was that, I just gave him Stafford and I was released."

Contractually, however, LaVoie was still committed to working on the second Jim Stafford album, *Not Just Another Pretty Foot*.

The sessions, held in Los Angeles, stretched out over several weeks. "Nobody said a word to me in the studio," LaVoie recalled. "Not Gernhard. Not Stafford. And I took Stafford to him! But I had to be there, to be the producer."

Not Just Another Pretty Foot was released within weeks of *A Cowboy Afraid of Horses*, the very last Lobo album. Lobo's final Gernhard-produced hit, reaching Number 27 in late April, was titled "Don't Tell Me Goodnight."

Before things between them had gone south, Gernhard and LaVoie entered into another kind of business venture. Back in Sarasota, Boyd Gernhard now had a realtor's license, and somehow convinced his son to invest in a land deal he had going. "I'll double your money in six months," the old man promised. Phil and Kent, separately, each forked over $20,000.

Boyd, for once, was as good as his word. "It was totally legitimate," LaVoie said. "He took us out to see the property and everything. Phil's mother was there but didn't say a word."

A year later, "I had to go to Sarasota for the closing, and Bud's going on and on about 'I made you all this money' and blah blah blah, but he made a 20 percent commission going in and out.

"He goes in to get the papers, and Phil's mother is sitting over there in a chair. A little meek woman. And she whispers 'Kent, have you seen Phil?' I said not recently, and she whispers 'If you see him, tell him his mother said hello.'

"And that summed it up. That guy was such a jerk. He was a real asshole."

Let Your Love Flow

"Looking back on it, it would've been nice if you'd had enough sense to say 'OK, this is not a fairy tale — I probably need a lawyer.' But I think a lot of people don't think like that — it's such a dream come true that you just take the ride."

Jim Stafford

After Stafford's "re-interpretation" of "Spiders and Snakes" became a smash, Gernhard was quick to solicit more songs from young David Bellamy.

He and Scotti cut a deal for David to record for Warner/Curb, and the single "Nothin' Heavy" — recorded in London during the Petula Clark sessions - was released early in 1975.

In the meantime, Gernhard got Howard Bellamy, who was spinning his wheels back in Florida, a job as a roadie for Jim Stafford; eventually, he would replaced Gallagher as road manager.

Not Just Another Pretty Foot, the second Stafford album (the result of the sessions wherein Kent LaVoie got the cold shoulder from everyone) included four songs with the writing credit "J. Stafford — D. Bellamy." Although the two writers were rarely in the same room.

"I did that with a few songs," said Stafford, "and some of them I don't think I really improved. I think 'You'll Never Take Me Alive' was probably

*Winter Haven's unstoppable one-man show, Jim Stafford, looking wacky for TV's **The Jim Stafford Show**, which aired in the summer of 1975. Gernhard was the variety hour's executive producer. ABC publicity photo.*

better the way he had it than the way I had it. And there might have been others that way.

"But you look at a guy like me, I'm out there, I'm getting lots of attention, sometimes you're not as smart as you think you are. Some of those songs of Dave's I was shaping, trying to fit out to be more like what I would do than what he would do.

"I made 'Spiders and Snakes' — at least for me — a better song, but Dave's a heck of a writer. There were some great songs in there."

But Stafford — and Gernhard, Scotti and Durgom - most certainly had bigger plans. The goal was to work Stafford into the Hollywood mainstream. On *In Concert, Midnight Special* and the other performance-based shows of the time, and on *The Bobby Goldsboro Show* and *The Tonight Show Starring Johnny Carson*, Stafford had come across as an affable guest and an extremely likeable performer.

His sort of humor played well on television, and that's where Bullets earned his Gernhard-Scotti salary: In May 1975, TV stars Dennis Weaver and Sandy Duncan, along with teen country singer Tanya Tucker and up-and-comer Jim Stafford, hosted *Timex Presents Opryland U.S.A.* on ABC, a 60-minute commercial for Nashville's new theme park. Subsequently, a deal was made for *The Jim Stafford Show,* a videotaped variety hour to air for six Wednesdays over the summer.

Gernhard and Scotti were executive producers of the program, to be developed and written by Rick Eustis and Al Rogers, the same team responsible for a recent series of John Denver specials. The "cast" included Valerie Curtin, Richard Stahl, Gallagher, the Carl Jablonski Dancers and young, doe-eyed Tennessee songbird Deborah Allen. Stafford traded barbs with a wisecracking sidekick, Rodney the Robot, and the "voice inside his guitar" was provided not by Gallagher, who did the honors in Stafford's stage show, but by cartoon legend Mel Blanc.

Except for the presence of Stafford himself, *The Jim Stafford Show* was virtually identical to every other cookie-cutter variety program in the mid '70s, ubiquitous on all three networks. Over its six weeks, Stafford played host to the likes of Gavin McLeod, Bernadette Peters, George Gobel and the Captain and Tennille.

"The likeable Stafford easily outdoes the canceled Mac Davis when it comes to being a down-home country boy and displays a greater feel for comedy than Tony Orlando," said a reviewer in the *Chicago Tribune*.

Ultimately, however, Tony Orlando got the last laugh. The summer series was not picked up for a regular run. And that fall, the premiere of *Saturday Night Live* sounded the death knell for old-school TV variety hours.

"Phil was in his element when he was producing records," Stafford said, "but as far as TV he was out of his comfort zone. He didn't know much about that. He didn't know much about what's entertaining to an audience. So we had to try to find me in the middle of all that stuff, to sort out what would work and what wouldn't work."

Gernhard often employed Neil Diamond's touring band, when they weren't out with the boss, for L.A. studio work. Drummer Dennis St. John thought Gernhard — always on the hunt for good songs — might like "Let Your Love Flow," written by his drum tech, Larry Williams. Diamond himself had politely passed on the tune.

Gernhard heard the song's potential immediately.

He took David Bellamy and the Diamond band into a Burbank studio and recorded the light-hearted, loping, country-esque pop song. But he wasn't satisfied with the result, feeling that David's version was missing something critical. He couldn't put his finger on it. So on the shelf it went. But it was never far from his thoughts.

He then flew to Florida to oversee a live segment for *The Jim Stafford Show* at the venerable Cypress Gardens water-skiing attraction in Winter Haven, Stafford's hometown. When dark clouds began to roll in, Gernhard instructed Stafford's audio crew to soundcheck the equipment on the outdoor stage so they could tape the segment quickly, before the rain fell.

A roadie strode onto the stage to test Stafford's microphone.

"Tony and I were standing there talking," Gernhard recalled, "and this voice drifted across from the other side of the lake where they were set up to shoot, and before I put two and two together, I said 'that's the voice for 'Let Your Love Flow.'" I turned around and it was Howard Bellamy, David's brother."

Back in L.A., he got together with Curb.

"Phil would rub the top of his moustache when he thought he had something really good," Curb laughed. "I don't think he realized he was doing that.

"But right after 'Who Loves You' by the Four Seasons was a hit, Phil said 'I bet you don't have a followup.' I said 'Yes, we do' — and it was 'Oh What a Night,' the next Four Seasons record. I played it for Phil, and he loved it.

"Then he said 'I have something to play for you.'" He rubbed his moustache.

"And he played me David's demo of 'Let Your Love Flow.' I told him I thought it sounded like a Doobie Brothers record. He told me that he liked the way Howard Bellamy sang it.

"I said 'We don't have Howard signed. He said 'Well, we can do it.'

"I said, 'What are they going to be called, David and Howard?' Phil said 'Let's record it. They could be the Bellamy Brothers. Or whatever.'"

And the Bellamy Brothers they were. It's often said in the record business that brotherly harmonies — rooted in the ties of blood, bone and a symbiotic growing-up — are the warmest, the closest, the most chill-inducing.

From the the Louvin Brothers to the Everly Brothers, from Tim and Neil Finn to Seth and Scott Avett, harmonizing brothers have created some spectacular and unforgettable music through the decades.

The Bellamys, of course, had been singing together all their lives, from Homer's knee at the Dade City Rattlesnake Roundup to their Gainesville frat-band days in Jericho.

"Howard was on the road with me for a long time," Stafford said. "I would tell the audience 'Hey, this guy and his brother have a song coming out — it's really great, and let's bring him up here to play it for you!' And Howard would come on with an acoustic guitar and sing 'Let Your Love Flow.'"

In the brothers' autobiography, David Bellamy told a different version of the story: He discovered the "Let Your Love Flow" demo among a stack of submitted tapes in Gernhard's office, while the producer was out.

On Jan. 31, 1976, "Let Your Love Flow" — the first recording by the newly-minted Bellamy Brothers — entered the Top 100 in *Billboard*. In early May it became Gernhard's second No. 1, after Maurice Williams and "Stay" 16 years earlier.

(As testament to Curb's own standing as a man with an ear for hits, the Four Seasons' "Oh What a Night" had already spent three weeks on top of the chart, in March.)

Gernhard told an interviewer he'd received letters from church groups, praising the Bellamy Brothers song's religious overtones. "What I envisioned was much more sensitive than that," he said. "I never thought about the religious aspect."

Said Curb: "Phil's production on that record ... it may be one of the greatest pieces of recorded music of all time."

Its gently galloping beat was like a breath of fresh county air in those strobe-lit days of disco, and in short order "Let Your Love Flow" reached audiences around the world aching for that same breath: It was a massive hit in a dozen countries, including Germany, where it spent five weeks on top.

As with everything done under the Gernhard-Scotti umbrella, the "Let Your Love Flow" label read *Produced by Phil Gernhard and Tony Scotti.* "I don't know what the deal was that the Scottis cut with Phil," Stafford said, "but I think they were very aware that he had some kind of gift for producing."

The Scotti Brothers' gift was promoting — making sure that the key people at the key radio stations knew that the latest Warner/Curb release was something they *needed* to play. A promotion man "worked" a record, making the calls, schmoozing the program directors, doing what it took to "break" a record in the markets that mattered, where airplay inevitably led to requests, which led to airplay in additional markets. Which — in a perfect world — led to national radio saturation, national record sales and lots of money in lots of pockets.

"Phil was doing all the production," explained Triplett. "I know, because I was the person booking the studios and the musicians. The Scottis were merely promoting, along with whatever Mike Curb's involvement was at the time. Other than some deal made, Tony Scotti didn't actually do any hands-on production. It was all Phil."

David Bellamy: "That sold a couple of million records, and Phil suggested that we should move out to L.A. I didn't want to at first, but when we started making money from the sales of that record, I knew things would be pretty good in L.A."

At home in Florida, Kent LaVoie got a copy of the "Let Your Love Flow" single in the mail. He liked the record well enough, but when he flipped it over, he was surprised to see that the B-side, "Inside of My Guitar," was credited to David Bellamy and Jim Stafford.

"Back then," LaVoie said, "that was maybe 10 or 12 grand for the flip side of a million seller. It wasn't any big money. But I called my publisher, Sid Herman, and I said 'That's a nice deal.' And he says 'Ohhh ... that was a mistake. You're not publisher on that.' I said 'What do you mean? ... it's *Stafford*.'"

"And he says 'Phil has a different agreement with us on songs that Jim doesn't record.' He went behind my back and made a deal, when I took it to him! If I'd have been in the room when I found that out, I would've killed him."

Once they came west from Florida, David and Howard Bellamy moved into the ground floor of the Hollywood Hills home, two rooms over from Gallagher. Stafford and Calder were on the upper level. "The heater was in my part, so I could hear Jim and Madeline argue ... sometimes about me," Gallagher said.

In short order, Madeline moved out, and Stafford began a relationship with Deborah Allen, the pretty young singer from his TV cast.

They were wild times, according to Stafford. "If success just slugs you, I think that you don't always behave good," he said. "Everything's easy. And so there were lots of women, and parties, and famous people all over the place."

The Bellamys' debut album for Warner/Curb, *Bellamy Brothers (Featuring "Let Your Love Flow" and Others)* was released in April. One of the tracks was "Nothin' Fancy," and it was the same master recording from London that had already been released as a solo David Bellamy single.

The brothers made the usual rounds of TV appearances, put together a band of their own and toured incessantly (particularly in Europe,

Hollywood nights: Gernhard, notoriously camera-shy, was most certainly at the table when this photo was taken in 1976: Madeline Calder, left, Jim Stafford and Deborah Triplett. From the collection of Madeline Calder.

where they were instant superstars because of the single's success).

Almost immediately, however, their relationship with Gernhard deteriorated.

After "Let Your Love Flow," David Bellamy told *People* magazine, "we hit bottom because we lost control. We had people working for us we didn't know, and managers wouldn't let us do our own music. We ended up in debt because of that record." Added his brother: "There were so many fingers in the pie that there was no pie left."

"We learned not to trust a damn soul in the business," Howard reflected.

From their book: "Gernhard had power of attorney over us, so we'd send the tour money back and we'd never see it when we got home. They'd have beach houses in Malibu, and we were basically broke."

They'd had the biggest record in the world. "By that time," David wrote in *Let Your Love Flow*, "Gernhard was hardly speaking to us except to get our money."

After *Plain and Fancy,* a second Gernhard-produced album, the Bellamy Brothers severed their ties with Gernhard, Scotti and Kaiser Music (a song from this album, the Dick Holler-penned "Crossfire," gave them another major hit in Europe, although it didn't chart Stateside).

"Phil did the second album, but then he turned it over to Michael Lloyd," said Curb. "Phil might have retained some publishing interests at that point.

"It's not that Phil is wrong, or the artist is wrong, it's just that his expectation there might not have been met. I thought they had a good relationship, but obviously not."

Said Deborah Triplett: "He *made* the Bellamy Brothers. I seem to recollect that Phil owned a lot of their publishing, and that might've pissed them off.

"But to defend Phil, why would he have done all this work? I always thought that he was smart that way — that he didn't just produce artists, he owned in most instances some of the publishing. Not all of it, but part of it."

Opined Stafford: "I think it was common with him and the bunch that he was with. That's sort of how they operated. They would set it up in a way that you were gonna get this this and this, and they were gonna get that and that ... basically, they got the lion's share. And that's just how it was."

David and Howard began to cater their songs, and their records, to the country market. They landed their first country No. 1, David's "If I Said You Had a Beautiful Body, Would You Hold it Against Me" in 1979, produced by Michael Lloyd, on Warner/Curb.

"Phil told me one time that he didn't like the 'Beautiful Body' thing," Stafford recalled. "Because he felt that if they'd left the steel guitar out, they'd have had a pop hit. That's what Phil told me. He said the country-fied version of it made it a country hit, but it could've been a crossover."

The Bellamys moved back to the family ranch in Florida, where they hired their mother, Frances, to keep the books (she even managed to cajole more money out of Gernhard).

Howard and David both raised large families on the ranch, and continued to raise market cattle for many decades, at the same time they were becoming one of the biggest-selling duos in country music history, riding the road hard.

Over the ensuing years, they re-corded their first — and biggest — hit, eventually all but erasing the original Gerhard arrangement.

Stafford put some thought into that. "Listen to 'Let Your Love Flow,' that's a good example of taking a song that everybody knew was a hit, but nobody knew what to do with," he said. "Why wouldn't he have given it to Dave Bellamy? He was the guy. Instead, Howard gets it.

"Dave wrote the songs and Dave sang the songs, and that's how he wanted it. So I don't think there's any love lost there. I know *I* don't get calls from those guys."

Not Just Another Pretty Foot wasn't the last album issued on MGM Records, but it might as well have been. Although *Jim Stafford* had peaked at a respectable — if not spectacular — No. 55 on Billboard's long-player chart, its successor never cracked the Top 200. The album got lost in the shuffle when European conglomerate PolyGram, which had purchased MGM, re-assigned the existing MGM artists and catalog to its Polydor Records subsidiary.

The album's disappearing act was hastened by the non-performance of two singles: The first, "Your Bulldog Drinks Champagne," a Stafford-Bellamy "collaboration," only got to No. 24.

Another small controversy surrounded the second, Stafford's cover of Shel Silverstein's "I Got Stoned and I Missed It" (which eked into the Top 40).

Phil and Tony took out an ad in *Billboard*:

Jim Stafford, Phil Gernhard and Tony Scotti acknowledge that the lyrics in the version of "I Got Stoned and I Missed It" as recorded by Jim Stafford on MGM Records is different from that version written by Shel Silverstein, the author of "I Got Stoned and I Missed It" and to the extent that the Jim Stafford version was changed from the original version without Mr. Silverstein's consent, they regret the change ... No claim of ownership, authorship or entitlement to writer's royalties was made by Jim Stafford with respect to such version.

Stafford wasn't new to "altering" other people's songs — as David

Bellamy found out — but he'd also red-penned Silverstein before. On his self-published 1971 album *Live at the Elbow Room*, a recording of his nightclub act at the time, Stafford performed Silverstein's "A Boy Named Sue," made famous a few years earlier by Johnny Cash.

Stafford's version was played for cheap laughs. When rough-and-tumble "Sue" meets his father, with murder on his mind for saddling him with such a feminine name, the two start lisping at each other in over-the-top, exaggerated "homosexual" lingo. Dad evens sings "Hello Dolly" to the boy.

To Stafford's credit, the bar crowd at the time found it a laugh riot.

Gernhard was still one hundred percent in the Jim Stafford business, arranging his TV appearances and trying to secure him a record deal now that MGM, for all intents and purposes, no longer existed.

A one-off deal with Polydor resulted in "Jasper," a story-song about a backwoods lothario infamous for sleeping with other men's wives. Although it echoed the spooky bayou atmosphere of "Swamp Witch," Stafford's first hit, the record — whose label, significantly, did not bear the names Scotti, Lobo or Curb - was not successful.

Next, he and Stafford co-produced a Warner/Curb single for Stafford's girlfriend, Deborah Allen. "Do You Copy," a love song written in CB radio lingo (a big craze in 1976) did not register.

Allen would go on to have a number of country hits, without Stafford or Gernhard involvement, in the 1980s.

Two Stafford singles on Warner/Curb were next, both of them suitably bizarre: "Turn Loose of My Leg" and "You Can Call Me Clyde."

Phil also managed to convince a skeptical Kent LaVoie — now living in Malibu - to put their past difficulties behind and try to re-capture lightning in a bottle by cutting a pair of Lobo singles for the label; like the Stafford attempts, both "Afterglow" and "You Are All I'll Ever Need" came and went with nary a ripple.

"Phil was very Hollywood," said LaVoie. "He was 'Let's take my Rolls to the studio.' Fairyland, you know? We weren't buddies, but we'd had a good thing and thought maybe we could keep it alive. We cut a couple of really nice records, but I had passed on. It was over.

"The superstars stay around. I was never a superstar. I probably wouldn't have been if I'd had 20 hit records."

And so, with nary a whimper, another partnership ended.

Curb, meanwhile, ran for the California lieutenant governor's seat in 1978 — and would serve, under Governor Jerry Brown, through 1983.

While he was away playing politics in Sacramento, Curb had issued a dictum to his label president, Dick Whitehouse: If Phil expresses an interest in producing anybody, any artist, just make it happen. Give him what he wants.

Rock superstar Jackson Browne had included a rendition of Maurice Williams' "Stay" on his multi-platinum *Running on Empty* album, and Gernhard was drawn to another song on the longplayer, a rocking Browne original called "You Love the Thunder."

He asked to produce it as a one-off single for country singer Hank Williams Jr., who'd been with Mike Curb since his days at the helm of MGM Records. In the late '70s, Curb Records was trying to turn Williams into a star, in the wake of a near-fatal mountain-climbing accident that left him disfigured and miserable. He was looking for a strong new image.

Gernhard waxed a Williams-sung rendition of "You Love the Thunder," and although it showcased his strong baritone voice on a song about male sensitivity, that wasn't the sort of thing country fans were snapping up in those days. The record stiffed.

The B-side, Williams' own "I Just Ain't Been Able," was subsequently included on his Curb album *Family Tradition*. This hard-nosed collection — credited to three different producers - proved to be just the introduction the newly rough and rowdy Williams needed, as it climbed to No. 3 and became the second gold album of his career (more, and more significant, successes were to come for the son of country music's most iconic figure).

For a while, Stafford remained Phil's primary point of focus. In a January, 1978 profile, Fred Wright of the *St. Petersburg Times* wrote:

Stafford and Gernhard have become street-wise in California and have learned how to deal and barter and play the game of celebrity politics. Now there are more conversations about television specials and variety series and situation comedies and feature films. Jim Stafford's star is on the rise again.

Florida, it seemed, was still on Gernhard's mind. In the newspaper piece, he announced that he was in the planning stages of a $1.5 million, 100,000-square-foot "restaurant-showroom complex" in St. Petersburg, to be Stafford's home base when we wasn't playing in Las Vegas or on the road somewhere.

Gernhard told the *Times* that the place, when it opened late in 1979, was to include a main showroom (with seating for up to 250), a semi-private restaurant, a private dining room and a semi-private disco.

The showroom, he said, would also serve as an out-of-town stage for "different people who don't normally come through the area and want to try out new things and material but not in Los Angeles."

When the showroom was dark, the restaurant and disco would be for members only.

"The combination of private and semi-private facilities basically seems to the something the area needs," Gernhard explained. "A place people can go and not contend with crowds."

The project never got off the ground, however. In 1978, Stafford met "Ode to Billie Joe" singer Bobbie Gentry, who'd just been signed to a lucrative Warner/Curb deal. In short order, they were married, a Gentry single was issued, they divorced, and Gentry gave birth to a son named Tyler. And that was that.

He and Gernhard didn't have an official partnership to dissolve. They simply stopped working together.

Stafford was hired to host the series *Those Amazing Animals* with Burgess Meredith and Priscilla Presley, and rode the charts one last time with a song from the Clint Eastwood movie *Any Which Way You Can*, produced by someone else.

Although it was an amicable split, Stafford recalled, "I think it would be fairly safe to say we weren't even friends. He saw the value in what I was doing and thought he could make some money. Or however you want to look at that. We were kind of thrown in together. But I don't know too many people that hang with their producers. If they do, that's a nice thing."

Stafford eventually sued and won back the publishing on his songs. When things were happening, he said, "I really didn't think about it. I didn't care much about all of that. I figured 'Well, that's what he does, he gets that money; I'm the performer, I'll get my money.' I didn't worry about it.

"You would've had to have been there in that time period, having all that attention. A guy just out of playing these little joints, and all of a sudden you're doing lots of TV work and all kinds of stuff you'd never dreamed of doing. So you can look back and say 'Man, I let a lot of money get away,' but when you start looking at the divorces and the women and all the stuff that went down ... somebody's always ready to take the money."

According to Stafford, Gernhard told him he'd been "screwed" by the junior-high deals he'd made with "Stay," his first hit. "So he went back to school and learned about the law. Because he wasn't ever gonna let that happen again.

"This is what made Phil what Phil was: He didn't want to ever get screwed again, so he learns enough about the law not to. But even though he knew how bad it was to get screwed, it was OK for him to screw people."

Lookin' For a Hit

SNUFF — "(So This is) Happy Hour" - The group's music falls in the vein of the Eagles, Poco and the Everly Brothers, with elements of traditional beach music. Snuff has built a regional following during the past five years, tallying more than 100 concert dates per year, in venues from New York to South Carolina. Their debut single was produced by Phil Gernhard, as is their debut self-titled LP on Elektra/Curb.

Billboard
"New on the Charts"
Aug. 14, 1982

Tony Scotti had been visiting England in the spring of 1978, and he came back with what he knew, absolutely knew, was a hit song. "Fool (If You Think it's Over)" by British singer/songwriter Chris Rea had a languid, champagne-and-cocaine groove, the sort of slinky arrangement that American groups like Pablo Cruise and Atlanta Rhythm Section were sending up the trade magazine charts at the time.

Best of all, Rea's version had flopped in the U.K., which meant nobody was scrambling to score the first stateside cover.

Gernhard placed the song with the House Band, an energetic Los Angeles rock outfit fronted by a wiry 22-year-old singer named James House.

He signed the House Band to a three-single deal with Warner/Curb, with an option on an album should the first single — "Fool (If You Think it's Over)" — turn to gold.

Before the record's release, Gernhard changed the band's name to Prisoner.

House hated that name (and he didn't think much of Chris Rea's song, either), but here were Phil Gernhard and Tony Scotti, music business veterans, dangling the career carrot out in front of him.

House didn't find Gernhard particularly soft and cuddly, but when they met to record that first single, the young musician was in for a surprise.

"Phil was like a different guy in the studio," he recalled. "He was like a kid in a candy store. He genuinely loved music. It was the first time I was ever exposed to somebody who could be that dark and love music so much.

"Because to me, music just makes life worth living, you know? And to see this Phil Spector-ish kind of guy was ... interesting."

The label rushed Prisoner's record to radio ... just as United Artists, which had licensed Chris Rea's music, released the songwriter's own version of "Fool (If You Think It's Over)" in the United States.

Unlike Rea's countrymen, American audiences loved the song. Rea's version raced up the charts, peaking at No. 12 in September. It was a No. 1 "Easy Listening" hit as well.

The Prisoner version? Not so much.

House, however, was a fool if he thought his relationship with the mercurial Gernhard and the thuggish Scotti was over. He'd signed a contract.

The second Prisoner single, *Hot Summer Night*, strove for that Bruce Springsteen-esque "sexy thrills on the night streets" appeal. It flopped, as did the third, an uptempo remake of the Otis Redding soul ballad "Try a Little Tenderness."

Phil was doing what he and Jimmy McCullough had perfected in the South Carolina era: Throwing everything at the wall in hopes that *something* would stick.

James House, who would have a successful career in country music in the 1990s, said the whole Gernhard/Scotti experience made him feel like a commodity, not an artist.

"My dad always said, 'Don't get involved with the bad guys in the business,' and the next thing I know, I'm hanging with the bad guys. He was the dark side of the music business."

Every aspect of the record industry was changing, none moreso than the preferences of consumers. They weren't buying "just" singles any more — more specifically, although there were still plenty of hit singles whose success was driven by radio play, they were nearly always presented as short previews of the bigger package — the album.

Although the top-selling album of 1977, *Saturday Night Fever*, produced six massively successful singles, the album sold 15 million copies and sat on top of the *Billboard* chart for an astonishing 24 consecutive weeks.

Hit singles from other period juggernauts — Fleetwood Mac's *Rumours*, Billy Joel's *The Stranger* and *52nd Street*, or *Hotel California* by the Eagles — sent album sales soaring.

Gernhard's method was decidedly old school, one single at a time. He'd sharpened his tools in the hit-driven days of AM radio and had never had much success with albums.

Still, he tried to adapt. After Michael Lloyd had produced a non-charting single for Arrogance, a rock 'n' roll band out of Chapel Hill, N.C., Gernhard went to Curb president Whitehouse and said he wanted to produce them. The deal was bumped-up to album length, and Gernhard went to work.

Arrogance, fronted by songwriters Robert Kirkland, Don Dixon and Rod Abernathy, was known around the Carolinas for its high-energy shows and thrilling vocal harmony blend.

"We were caught between being a coliseum rock act and a British pub-rock band, and I'm not sure Phil ever quite figured that connection out," said Dixon, who was also the group's bass player. "I know the people at Warner/Curb didn't understand it at the time, because their biggest hit before that had been 'You Light Up My Life' by Debby Boone or something."

Nevertheless, Gernhard — with carte blanch from Mike Curb - threw himself into the project. The band attended several pre-production meetings at the Gernhard-Scotti offices in California.

"That was always kind of an exciting and scary place to be," said Dixon. "The Scottis came from the old hard-nosed, New Jersey payola, strong-arm promotion days. But not like 'We're gonna beat you up,' more like the 'Here's some hookers and blow' kind of promotion days.

"Friendly, but 'If we give you X, we expect Y.' That was very clear. They had the 'If you agree to something, you better live up to it' type of reputation. Because they were totally independent, they could put money anywhere they wanted to, to break something. The paper trail was different than it would have been had they been at the heart of the Warner Brothers operation."

But the production deal was with Gernhard alone, and the members of Arrogance liked him. "He was totally into the song," Dixon recalled. "It wasn't like he thought he could market just any song or any voice.

"He had your classic record company dude look for the time — a little van dyke, a cigar and a nice gold ring. He definitely looked like he fit with the Scotti brothers, when I would go over to the office with him."

The *Suddenly* album was recorded, at Gernhard's insistence, at Reflection Sound Studios in Charlotte, on the band's home turf. They had recorded there before, and he knew they'd be more relaxed.

Although he seemed to be drinking all the time, Dixon said, Gernhard was focused and very much in command during the sessions. "I don't think he was a particular taskmaster. I think he wanted to get his way because he wanted to have a hit.

"If you're the producer and you're not opinionated, you're worthless. So I totally respected that side of him. In hindsight, I've always thought that he had a better idea of what the band really was than I did — the appeal and the dynamic and the potential of the band. When you're inside the band, you can't see it."

The members of Arrogance also liked Deborah, who was around for many of the sessions because she had family in Charlotte.

"I had to go pick up something from his hotel room," recalled Dixon. "We're in Charlotte; Deborah's in L.A., and I knew that somebody had come out to visit him. He'd said he had to go pick somebody up at the airport.

"Elke Sommer answers the door of his hotel room. She's wearing a bathrobe.

"When we went into the studio I said 'Man that was Elke Sommer!'

And he said 'Yeah, we've known each other a long time.' And that's all he ever said about it. He was very discreet. It was nudge-nudge-wink-wink."

Dixon, who would go on to a long and successful career as a record producer in his own right (R.E.M., the Smithereens, Guadalcanal Diary), said he enjoyed late-night talks with Gernhard in the control room. There, he heard all the stories — from Maurice Williams to the Royal Guardsmen, to Gernhard's discovery of the Bellamy Brothers to their bitterness and defection.

"You don't get something for nothing," said Dixon. "Maybe you gave your publishing to him in order to have a career. People can say what they want to about 'stealing,' but if you don't have a hit, you got nothing anyway. I bet Phil earned the publishing that he took.

"He certainly made a publishing deal for us that gave him half of our publishing, but I think we got fairly compensated, and I think it was a smart deal for us. And I have no regrets about those songs being co-published by Phil's publishing company at the time."

After a five-year courtship, Phil Gernhard and Deborah Triplett were married on Dec. 6, 1980 at Mike and Linda Curb's Hidden Valley ranch, in the Santa Monica mountains.

By then, she'd had a drunken earful about Boyd and Sara, back home in Sarasota. Phil, she discovered, had been making loans to the old man to help him with his real estate deals.

She never really understood the love/hate dynamic between Phil and his father. "I met them once," Triplett said. "They came to Los Angeles and we all went to dinner. And it was clear that they didn't like me. I don't know why not! They just weren't welcoming to me at all.

"And he broke it off with them not too long after that dinner. There was a phone discussion about buying some property in Florida. And there was a big, big fight. That night, he shut them out."

After the Arrogance experience, Gernhard championed a Richmond, Virginia sextet called Snuff. He liked the band's polished harmonies — he'd been a sucker for close harmonies ever since the days of Dick Holler and the Holidays, who'd left Baton Rouge, appeared in Columbia and proceeded to become the most popular band in town because, as Holler liked to boast, they could sing rock 'n' roll harmonies better than any of those homegrown Carolina shag-dance bands.

The sessions took place at Electric Lady in New York, which Gernhard

Dec. 6, 1980: Phil and Deborah wed at the Curb Ranch in Hidden Valley, Calif. Bullets Durgom is standing behind Phil; behind the bride are Mike and Linda Curb. From the collection of Deborah Triplett.

had first used back in 1971, for "Me and You and a Dog Named Boo." An entire album was recorded — and the 24-track master tapes were subsequently ruined by a studio engineer who inadvertently used them while calibrating the machine, superimposing a test tone over the entire, expensive project.

Gernhard sued the studio for $500,000 for gross negligence, claiming that "delaying placement of the master tapes with a label will result in Gernhard's loss of his option with Snuff due to the time period outlined in his agreement with them."

This settlement in hand, Gernhard block-booked Alpha Audio in downtown Richmond. He rented a place for himself and another for California-based engineer Ron Saint Germain, who was hired to assist.

As with the Arrogance sessions, it was clear from Day One that Gernhard was the boss. "I would recuse myself from the control room during the mixdown, because he was very much in control of any project he was in," recalled Chuck Larson, Snuff's singing/songwriting frontman. "What he said went, and that's the way it was. He was an absolute producer — you did it his way, or you didn't do it."

Like father, like son.

"I'm not saying he was bellicose," Larson insisted. "He was very quiet, but he had definite ideas on everything and that's pretty much the way it was."

And despite his proficiency at the board, Gernhard didn't always get it right. "Sure, he had a sense about what was good music, but at the same time had kind of a heavy hand to where he would destroy what he was making," according to Larson.

In other words, he occasionally *over*-produced — dubbing in so many vocal harmonies, for example, that the track began to sound artificial -but was astute enough to realize it and pull back.

They spent weeks together in Richmond, piecing together the *Snuff* album, which Gernhard — not surprisingly — placed with Curb, under its latest affiliation, with Elektra Records (the label went totally independent in 1983, once Curb exited the lieutenant governor's office).

Like Don Dixon, Larson had many long talks with the famous producer. "Phil had almost an obsessive nostalgia for the doo-wop era, and he was always trying to capture some feeling he had in his youth," Larson said.

"I think he was one of those people who spent a lot of time alone, and he was very much a romantic. There was always some kind of an air of regret that you could sense about Phil. He was breathlessly looking for something."

He might have been looking for trouble when he ventured into one of the city's seedier neighborhoods. "One night, Phil had his car parked out in the alley," Larson remembered. "He always carried a gun in his briefcase. This guy comes up to his window, pulls a knife and says 'Give me your money.' Phil says 'It's in my briefcase.'

"He opens his briefcase, pulls out the gun and sticks it in the guy's face and says 'Is this enough?'"

Snuff was released in 1982 on Elektra/Curb, and while it moved 40,000 copies in Virginia and North Carolina — in areas the band toured frequently and had amassed followings — on a national level, it stiffed.

In '83, Gernhard was back for Snuff's second album. Somehow, *Night-Fighter* — which focused on the band's harder, rockier side, rather than the country/rock of the debut — was released as a six-song EP, sort of a

With Virginia's Snuff, 1981, celebrating the band's signing to Elektra Records. Snuff would be the final artist Gernhard (second from right) would produce. Photo from the collection of Chuck Larson.

half-album. It's conceivable that Curb, which was severing ties with Elektra in the run-up to becoming a fully independent label — was simply washing its hands of another failed artist, and turned off the finance faucet.

Whatever the reason, Snuff, and *NightFighter*, got no promotion and were abandoned by the label.

Not that Gernhard hadn't poured all of his talent and studio expertise into the project.

"I think he had a lot of pressure to continually produce hits," explained Larson. "I don't think you can really tell a story about Phil Gernhard without Mike Curb in it. He was more or less Mike's production lieutenant, for lack of a better word.

"Phil would give me an amalgamation of what program directors were looking for, and then I was supposed to come up with their ideas as he saw them. Whether it's right or wrong, it was hard for me, because I'm an old hippie songwriter."

"In Snuff, I really think Phil saw another Eagles. But we could never,

ever get it right in the studio. He said to me one time 'If this project doesn't go well, I may have some serious career problems.'"

Although he remained a key Curb employee for the rest of his life, after *NightFighter* Phil Gernhard never produced another record.

"Phil never had friends, and that was one of the problems with our relationship," said Deborah Triplett. "He had so much invested in me that when I hurt him, it really cut him deep. So deep that he almost couldn't forgive me for it."

To this day, she feels a tremendous sense of guilt and regret for a moment of infidelity in the early '80s, during Gernhard's time with Snuff. "He even went to therapy with me for a while, to try to work through it," Triplett said. "But he just hit a point where he said 'Deborah, I can't do this because I can't stop seeing it in my mind.'"

The divorce was finalized in 1984. "Part of our problem also was that Phil was an alcoholic," she explained. "That played into the breakup of our marriage also.

"He told me once that he drank so that he could feel more socially comfortable, because the truth was that when he did drink he WAS more socially comfortable. But Phil didn't like bullshit. In life, you've got to do a lot of bullshit to ingratiate yourself in the world."

Eventually, Triplett moved back to North Carolina and settled in Charlotte. "I can't speak for the other women," she said, "but when I was with him I felt like there were two things that were important in his life: Me and music."

It would be a full two years before Phil would even speak to her again.

You either drag
or you get drug

"We talked a lot after he moved to Nashville — in fact, he even asked me to re-marry him. Twice. And he wasn't drunk at the time."

Deborah Triplett

Most of Curb Records' successes in the 1980s were with country music artists. Through imprint deals with various labels, Curb had championed the Judds, Sawyer Brown, Desert Rose Band, Exile, Lyle Lovett, Sawyer Brown, Hal Ketchum and others.

The pop division wasn't doing nearly as well, nor was Curb's foray into movies (*Mac and Me, Voyage of the Rock Aliens, Body Slam, Bikini Island*) breaking any box office records.

Gernhard, grappling with his addictions and staying away from the studio, wasn't involved with a lot of it. "There was no life except work for a while there," he reflected in a 1988 interview with his hometown paper, the *Sarasota Herald-Tribune*. "It was crazy, so I tried to simplify things by getting rid of some of my responsibilities.

"I try to be a trouble-shooter, listening to groups, working with musical writers, doing film treatments and picking scores."

He told the newspaper that he wanted to go back to school and earn a Ph.D in psychology within five years, in order to spend "my old age writing and doing research." Also in the works, he boasted, was a movie about his early days as a doo-wop producer.

Instead, Curb moved the entire company, lock, stock and recording studios, to Nashville's Music Row in 1992. With the occasional exception, Curb Records would be, from that moment on, a country label.

Phil Gernhard, of course, went with him, unwilling (or unable) to produce, but eager to do his part at the A&R (Artists & Repertoire) level — helping the label's artists find and record the best songs (for them) and put out records that would, first and foremost, get played on the radio stations that Curb's promotions department deemed the most significant.

The lines between A&R and promotion were frequently blurred when Gernhard — who was, for all intents and purposes, the bossman's golden boy — got serious about an artist.

As the senior man in Curb Records' A&R department — answering only to Mike Curb himself - he championed Louisiana singer Tim McGraw, whose father was "Tug" McGraw, a former star pitcher for the New York Mets and, later, the Philadelphia Phillies.

In `92, just as Gernhard was settling in to his office in Curb's new Nashville headquarters, he was presented with a rough mix of McGraw's in-progress second album. The singer's eponymously-titled debut had been a resounding flop, but the label still had high hopes they had a male singer who could compete on the platinum-sales level of Capitol's Garth Brooks and Arista's Alan Jackson.

Byron Gallimore, McGraw's co-producer (with James Stroud), received a call out of the blue from the mighty Gernhard, whom he had yet to meet. "He was raving about the record we'd done," Gallimore recalled. "He would always talk in a quiet, whispery voice when he was excited. He said 'I've just got a question for you — I want to know how y'all did this.' And I'm like, 'What do you mean?'

And he said 'Listen, I like 10 of these 11 songs. And I don't like *nothin*.'"

Oh, thought Gallimore. *Tell me more.*

"And I remember distinctly that he said to me 'This is going to be Tim McGraw's year.'"

Gernhard made Tim McGraw and his album — eventually titled *Not a Moment Too Soon* — his top priority. Even though it was McGraw's sophomore effort, it had to be treated as the first time fans, radio and the

February 1984: The one and only time Gernhard accompanied Mike Curb to Daytona for the NASCAR races. Here, they congratulate driver Daryl Watrip on his victory (driving the Curb-sponsored car) in the Busch Grand Nationals. Curb Records.

entertainment media were getting a look at the guy — first impressions being all-important in pop culture.

"I think he was a master at picking singles, and hearing talent, and knowing what would work," Gallimore said. "He was a master at songs, too, because that's part of it, picking the right songs for singles.

"On Tim, he wasn't in the middle of the song search so much as he was picking what to do, picking what was a hit and making sure those things went well for him."

Gernhard chose "Indian Outlaw" as the first single. Written by Tommy Barnes, it was an uptempo song with lyrics stringing together a series of Native American clichés ("wigwam," "medicine man," "my arrow and my hickory bow" et cetera). The narrator was also the titular character, "Half Cherokee and Chocktaw," but his friends called him "Bear Claw."

"Too many record guys would've been afraid to go with it, because they thought radio wouldn't play it," said Gallimore. "Knowing what would work in radio back then, and what wouldn't, this song was out of the stack just a little bit. Phil was taking a chance. I think he viewed it as a hit and didn't care."

John Anderson's "Seminole Wind," in a similarly minor key but with a much more reverential tone, had been a hit just a year before. Was country radio ready to whoop it up so soon with "Indian Outlaw"?

Ah, but Gernhard believed "Indian Outlaw" had that magical quality that generates airplay and record sales: Repeatability. Maybe it was just a tad gimmicky, but the melody and pounding rhythm of "Indian Outlaw" were impossible to ignore — once they got lodged in your brain, they were virtually impossible to shake loose. You looked forward to hearing it again.

And the last verse was a hoot: "They all gather 'round my teepee/Late at night tryin' to catch a peek at me/In nothin' but my buffalo briefs/I got 'em standin' in line."

It didn't hurt that McGraw had a sexy baritone voice and a dark, brooding look under his wide-brimmed black hat, which Gernhard brought to the fore in the song's official video.

"From the day I made the decision to go with the 'Indian Outlaw' cut as a single, I knew I would need to pound the beaches with the most spectacular

video possible before going to radio. (Video director) Sherman Halsey delivered exactly what I needed.

"In fact, I can guarantee without that video I could never have broken this record. I know that because the record broke out of the Southeast, where CMT (Country Music Television) has tremendous penetration. So many calls came into radio stations in that region, requesting the single, that we were virtually accused of hiring people to phone in requests. But it all came from the video. Sherman did a terrific job of catching the energy of the piece. He also nailed Tim from an imaging standpoint. Tim just leaps off the screen."

Phil Gernhard
Business Wire
March 28, 1994

Despite complaints from Native American groups that the lyrics to "Indian Outlaw" reinforced tired and offensive stereotypes, the single became one of the fastest-selling of 1994. It was also McGraw's first Top 40 entry, and rose to No. 8 on the *Billboard* country chart - and 15 on the pop chart.

"From my perspective, I give him total credit for breaking Tim and making 'Indian Outlaw' happen," Gallimore stressed. "Tim really believed in 'Indian Outlaw,' and I would've picked it too, but we were a bit naïve as far as what the marketplace was. We just liked it and thought it was a hit, but when Phil heard it he thought it was a smash and made it happen."

And with the introductions made, Tim McGraw exploded. His next single, "Don't Take the Girl," was also curated by Gernhard. It became the first No. 1 in what would turn out to be a very long and lucrative career for the singer. *Not a Moment Too Soon* was the top-selling country album that year.

"Tim broke so big for Curb, and so they were so nice to us," Gallimore explained. "They were just a great label to work for. Mike Curb was always awesome to me, too. Tim was their project, and it was a priority, whatever they needed to do to make it work."

Gernhard never stopped working on McGraw's behalf, and the hits stacked up — "Not a Moment Too Soon," "Down on the Farm," "I Like it, I Love It," "Can't Be Really Gone," "She Never Lets it Go to Her Heart." And in 1997, McGraw accomplished a rare feat: Four consecutive singles reached the top of the chart.

"He didn't sign Tim McGraw, but he played a huge role in Tim's career," said Curb. "For many years, Phil would call me and say 'Tim's got a new single I think we should look at.' Or someone would submit a song to me that I thought was good, and I'd put it in his mailbox on a Saturday night or a Sunday morning."

It was a very, very long hot streak. "We made fast friends," Gallimore said. "Phil was an unusual guy. People on Music Row never even saw him much; he just didn't hang out with many people.

"For some weird reason, he liked me, and he liked Missi, my wife. Missi did a lot of the song searching for Tim, and he had a lot of respect for her."

Sara Arnold Gernhard died in a Sarasota nursing home on April 10, 1995. Phil, who felt betrayed by both of his parents (Sara, for not standing up to Boyd, and Boyd, for being Boyd) hadn't spoken to them since that big blowup at the dinner table, in Deborah's presence.

Judee called to break the news. Phil coldly informed his sister he wasn't coming to the funeral. All right, she said, but you only get one chance to make this particular decision. "And if you don't go, you may regret it for the rest of your life," she told him. He capitulated.

And so the siblings were reunited for the first time in 20 years. "He showed up in a limo," Judee Gernhard said. "After the service at the Episcopal church, he came to my father's house, and he asked me to go for a ride with him.

"We rode around, and we went up to the Ringling Museum. We parked there, his driver got out and we talked for an hour.

"He blamed Dad for her death. He was very bitter about my mother. She died of emphysema, and heart complications. And he was still smoking in the friggin' house when my mother had oxygen on!"

But the worst was yet to come. Following their heart-to-heart in the Ringling Museum parking lot, Phil and Judee returned to the family home. There was Boyd, in his usual armchair, filling the air with cigarette smoke.

"Oh, the big music man is here," said the old man derisively.

Phil turned on his heel, got back in the limo and drove straight to the airport. "And that was the last time I ever saw him," said his sister.

Since his second divorce, Gernhard hadn't been having a lot of success with women. "Phil's expectations of his wives was that they would be perfect," Curb explained. "And Phil was always looking for artists that were grateful. His expectation of artists was that they would all come up and say 'Phil, you're great. Thank you so much for the hit.'

"I remember saying to him, 'Phil, you're kind of lucky you don't have kids, because they don't come up to you and tell you how great you are.' Particularly when they're teenagers, they don't say 'You're the greatest dad in the world!' Well, recording artists very rarely come up and say 'Wow, how great is this? Thank you so much for finding this song for me. Thank you for my career.' You don't hear that very often."

Gernhard's alcoholism, Curb said, never got in the way of his work. Privately, however, it was a different story.

"One night at dinner he started drinking," said Curb. "He got in the car and started driving home, and we followed him. He was pulled over by a policeman. The policeman said OK, do the ABC's, and Phil sang it 'A B C D E F G …' And that didn't go over well, obviously. But they released him. We were able to get him off."

He married Nashville attorney Patricia Young on May 28, 1994 — but the union was doomed from the start. "I remember on the night he got married to Pat," Curb continued. "We got our cars at the same time at the Loews Vanderbilt, and I looked over; he was smashed. I gave the valet 20 bucks to park his car, and told the guy we'd be back tomorrow to pick it up. Linda and I drove Phil home."

In February, during her engagement to Gernhard, Young had been sexually assaulted in her home by a man who came to be known as the Wooded Rapist; his m.o., over a spree that lasted more than a dozen years, was to attack women whose homes were adjacent to wooded areas. Wearing a ski mask, he committed his crimes in the wee hours on rainy nights, then slipped away into the trees. Gernhard was away at the time.

Young's experience was later chronicled on an episode of the NBC series *Dateline*.

During the attack, Young had the foresight to bite off a tiny piece of her attacker's hand, and to hide it under the bed while the man was otherwise occupied. That way, she thought, even if she were murdered — which seemed likely — police would have a sample of the rapist's DNA.

This became, understandably, the blackest moment of Pat Young's life. Unfortunately, she explained, her fiancé could not have been less supportive.

"Phil was an incredibly difficult person," reflected Young. "He didn't like himself very much, and that made it really hard to like him."

He'd told his girlfriend that he'd been in analysis for 10 years, during his last decade in California (according to Deborah Triplett, Phil started seeing a therapist when their marriage fell apart, in 1983).

The first warning light started flashing in the back of Pat Young's mind when he mentioned his time in analysis.

"The issue with Phil broke down after we became engaged, which was his idea," Young said. "In his mind, I went to the position of power, and he had to pare that back down. Up until then, he did the best he could.

"The theory, he told me, was 'In any relationship, there's a person that's emotionally stronger. And you either drag or you get drug.'

"Now, I don't know where that came from, but that's how he saw life. He told me that he was badly abused by his father; that both of his parents were alcoholics. And Phil was an alcoholic."

Because her attacker was not immediately identified, Gernhard "said some ridiculous things about it," according to Young.

Curb, succinctly, believed "they got divorced primarily because he couldn't handle the rape."

Young would only say that Gernhard "was more concerned about why there wasn't a support group for men in his position — why are all the groups for women? Why do the counselors only talk to the victims, what about him? In his eyes, the world revolved around him."

The arguments, which could turn vicious and cruel, began around the time they bought the big home on Hillview Drive in Brentwood, late in 1993.

For Young, her new husband's attitude was painful. During the attack, "I got hit in the face a lot, and my short-term memory wasn't very good. And my house was sold. And we'd already bought another house. So at that point, I felt stuck.

"By the time the honeymoon was over, I knew I'd made a dreadful mistake."

The couple's divorce was finalized a week shy of their second anniversary. He reimbursed her for her share of the house, and continued to live there until his death in 2008.

Internally, Young filed her brief union with Gernhard under "Bad Decisions," and rarely spoke with him after the divorce. "Phil had eggshell feelings," Young said. "If you said anything, if he thought your tone was wrong, you had been unkind and unloving. And yet he could say anything he felt like. To you, to your friends, to whoever. And that's just not a way to live."

Eventually, the Nashville area's most notorious serial rapist was caught, tried and convicted. Each of the 13 cases was tried separately. "He was convicted in my case of attempted aggravated rape, because he didn't finish what he started," said Young, who went public with her story not long after the incident. "But I had the living shit beat out of me. I was battered pretty good."

Robert Jason Burdick was sentenced — for the most recent of his awful crimes — to 23 years in prison, in April, 2008. Other convictions and sentences followed.

As the '90s progressed, Gernhard - officially titled Senior Vice President of A&R - continued to work in numerous capacities at Curb.

New England singer Jo Dee Messina had been cutting songs with Byron Gallimore, Tim McGraw's producer, when she accompanied him to Fan Fair, on of Nashville's biggest industry events, in 1995.

When Gallimore and McGraw introduced her to Gernhard, according to Nashville legend, the notoriously brassy Messina said to the A&R guru:

"So I was thinking, y'all need a redhead on your label!" When he heard her high-energy demos, Gernhard couldn't help but agree.

The results were more smash hits for Curb. Gernhard brought the song "Heads Carolina, Tales California" to Messina; issued as her first Curb single, it roared straight into the Top Ten. The album *Jo Dee Messina* went gold, its followup (*I'm Alright*) sold more than two million copies (making it a multi-platinum seller).

Mike Curb: "He understood the relationship between promotion and creativity, so he would follow through and find the right programmer to play it for, the right radio concept. He was the total record person, always looking. But always wishing that he could find an artist who would tell him 'this is great.'

"Because being a record producer is an art form, but a lot of people who produce records don't really do the whole thing — they just go into the studio for a couple hours and let the engineers do the rest. Phil did it all."

In early 2004, Tim McGraw's eighth album was nearly finished when Gernhard told the Gallimores he thought something was still missing from the project. At his suggestion, Missi got back into song search mode and returned with "Live Like You Were Dying," an anthemic, power-of-positive-thinking song by Tim Nichols and Craig Wiseman.

McGraw liked it, and cut it, and when the album was released in July of that year, it was titled *Live Like You Were Dying*. The single sat on top of the chart for seven weeks — it was the biggest seller of the year — and the album entered the Top 200 at Number One, selling more than four million copies.

Tim McGraw made Curb Records. Since planting itself in Nashville in the early '90s, the label had a scored with a solid fistful of successful artists, including LeAnn Rimes, Jo Dee Messina and Steve Holy, but none came within swinging distance of McGraw's 40 million records sold, 25 No. 1 singles and 10 chart-topping albums.

A lot of people made Tim McGraw a star, without question, including Mike Borchetta — the Curb executive who'd signed him to the label - Byron Gallimore, James Stroud, Mike Curb and, especially, Phil Gernhard.

Alone in his big empty house, Gernhard sometimes called both ex-wife Sandy and ex-wife Deborah, usually in the post-midnight hours, and always when he was well-lit with Jack Daniels.

He would hold forth on what was right or wrong in the world, in his view, then ask them what was new in their lives. He usually followed up with slurring, unsolicited advice on how they could make things better.

He almost always called back the next day and apologized. "After our divorce, I didn't know that other Phil too well," Sandy said. "It was scary. He would call me in the middle of the night saying 'Isn't this pitiful? You're the only friend I have to talk to.'"

When Deborah's beloved father passed away, Gerhard called the family home in North Carolina to offer his condolences to his ex-wife and her siblings.

Boyd Gernhard died in the summer of 2002, at the age of 93. Phil, predictably, did not fly home for the funeral.

Judee, by then, was living in California. "I hated going home after my mother was gone," she said. "I was scared to death of my father, still. I was very, very physically uncomfortable around him. I would revert to being 10 years old and wanting to run away to the Ringling Art Museum again.

"He changed his will so many times. First my daughter was out of it, then she was in. I remember him saying 'There's money in the will to pay back your damn brother. And it's with interest, so be sure to make sure he knows that.'

"And that was so hurtful. That was just his attitude. He didn't know how to be gracious. Not to us. We were the hidden abused."

And it never, ever let up, even after the old man was gone. "When Phil started making money, my father borrowed from him all the time. It was really awful. It was ugly.

"After he died, I discovered that he had leveraged the house probably 20 times, as a personal loan. He'd borrow $5,000 and put the house up against it. I didn't even know if we owned the friggin' house."

If You're Going Through Hell

"At the time, I didn't know his background. I'm glad I didn't — I probably would've been nervous as a cat. 'Let Your Love Flow' is on my Top Ten, all-time favorite list. Still, to this day, I love that record when I hear it."

Byron Gallimore

Phil Gernhard was a loner and a deeply private man. In his Nashville years, particularly after the painful end of his marriage to Pat Young, he kept to himself. Even those who thought of themselves as his "friends" had little idea what he did when he wasn't working.

He kept an office in the Curb building, but he was rarely there. He preferred to work from the big Brentwood house, rattling around in his bathrobe, doing business by email and telephone. Such was his place on the company totem pole that nobody questioned this practice. Whatever Phil wanted, Phil got. It was as simple as that.

In some offices, the mighty Gernhard was feared. If he didn't like something, he would tell you. Loudly.

Occasionally, he'd wander into a room where Curb staff writers and song pluggers were talking shop. "This was open season for Phil to rant and rave about how untalented everyone was," said one writer who wished to remain anonymous. "He was a pissed off, cruel little fucker. We all hated him.

"I have respect for him as a record man. He could master vinyl, produce, engineer … anything. But every writer at Curb wanted to beat his ass."

Said Rodney Atkins, the Georgia-born singer/songwriter who'd signed with Curb in the late 1990s: "I've heard people say that Phil was so blunt, he was like an icepick in the forehead with what he'd say."

After a recording session, Atkins recalled, "He'd say 'This is obviously a scratch vocal. Why are you playing me this?' after I'd spent two weeks doing the vocal.

"But the thing is, he was quick to tell you when you did something good. The life lesson with Phil was that you can't trust somebody's 'yes' until you can trust their 'no.' He really made it worthwhile to dig in and work."

It's likely Gernhard's alcohol and drug intake had worn away his inner monologue, affecting his ability to filter his words and function in social situations. It was, Curb explained, a problem that never fully went away.

"I can make it real simple: Phil never met any substance, alcohol or drugs, that he probably didn't try," Curb said. "And he never met one that he could control. He didn't have the ability to stop, so if he tried something one night, it could last six months or a year. He just didn't have that shut-off valve."

Curb, who'd always been a straight arrow — an anomaly in the music business — said Gernhard never told him exactly what he was hooked on at any given time. Curb, for his part, didn't want to know.

Once, drinking wine, Gernhard felt compelled to tell Curb about the miserable relationship he'd had with his father. He never could seem to shake it off.

There were times Curb suspected that Gernhard was high on some substance or other on one of the rare occasions they met socially. But never at work — in the office, and in the studio, Phil always seemed to be on top of his game.

However, "My experience was always that just when I thought Phil had taken a turn to be perfect, something would happen, and he would re-visit one of his demons," Curb explained. "And we'd go to work on it.

"It's kind of like having a brother. People would say to me 'How long are you going to keep working with Phil?' and I'd say 'Forever.' Because he gave so much to us, in terms of his passion and his talent, and sharing his life with us."

It was the addictions, Curb figured, that fueled Gernhard's decision to stop producing, and focus on A&R work, when the company was still based in Los Angeles back in the '80s. At times he seemed directionless, lost, in need of something intangible and just out of his reach.

Curb: "He'd say 'I'm not in very good shape.' I'd say 'Phil, what do we need? Do we need to get into some kind of program?' And he'd say 'No.'"

Since the '80s, Gernhard had been allowed to take six-month "sabbaticals," with pay. Even Curb wasn't certain where he disappeared to. "You're going to overcome this," Curb would tell his friend.

And always, Phil would come back to work.

A six-song demo CD from a teenage Swedish singer named Sofia Loell landed on his desk one day in 2001; it was bright, shiny, well-crafted dance-pop music, the sort of thing made by stars like Britney Spears and Katy Perry, and the likes of which Curb desperately needed for its flagging pop division.

Loell was summarily signed to Curb Records, for her American debut. The masters were leased from Stockholm-based Pama Records, Loell's domestic label, more songs were recorded to make a complete album, and Gernhard led the charge on breaking the artist on this side of the Atlantic.

Her *Right Up Your Face* album was released in the States midway through 2002.

Billboard raved:

Meet Sofia Loell, a Scandinavian import whose vocal texture conjures Alanis Morissette juiced up after a couple bars of chocolate. "Right Up Your Face" is an intriguing blend of alternative roots via Loell's scratchy vocals and introspective lyrics, swirled with a sunny melodic accessibility that shamelessly flirts with good ole pop.

Even in the days of the big-money promotion operatives, you couldn't buy copy like that, and the Curb team basked in it. If they still had the mojo, they would break Sofia Loell in America, and break her big.

Gernhard traveled to Stockholm that fall to oversee the video shoot for the first single released from *Right Up Your Face*. On set, he was introduced to Anna Maria Madeline Bosdotter Pettersson, a gorgeous, long-legged Swedish blonde, a blue-eyed Scandinavian beauty right out of Central Casting. She was working as Loell's makeup artist for the video shoot; she had a beautiful smile and a flirtatious way about her.

Pettersson was 28 years old. Gernhard was 61, desperately lonely - and smitten.

Just after Christmas, back in Nashville, Byron and Missi Gallimore were introduced to Phil's new wife, who spoke English through a thick Scandinavian accent. They'd been married in a quickie Las Vegas ceremony.

Her name, she said, was Maria.

Curb never met the fourth Mrs. Gernhard, whose limited Swedish visa only allowed her to visit America for six weeks at a time. "Every day was a new day with Phil," he said. "Usually, when he was going through a tough time and was on the winning side of it, or was getting off whatever he shouldn't have been on in the first place, there'd be a new Phil: 'I don't think I want to produce any more. I want to do A&R administration.' 'Hey, I want to go to Oxford.' 'Hey, I've fallen in love.'

"Oh boy — that was the one. Anything he said, other than 'I'm falling in love,' made me happy. Because I knew when he said 'I'm falling in love,' we were in for a ride."

Although Sofia Loell and *Right Up Your Face* didn't click with American audiences, Gernhard had a good feeling about the brand-new 21st century — once his beautiful young wife got her green card, she could live with him permanently in the brick house in Brentwood.

He told his friends he was putting her through school in Stockholm, and that they were planning a big, formal, second wedding in Nashville. During one of his inebriated late-night phone calls, he told his sister he desperately hoped to finally father a child.

Gernhard hired Kelly Lynn, a friend of Byron and Missi Gallimore's, as his assistant. The former Country Music Association "trophy girl" (she handed the awards to the winners as they walked onstage during the televised ceremony, while "smiling and looking pretty") had worked on the fringes of the music industry, and was interested in learning more.

With Gernhard, she got an education.

"From the minute I met Phil, it was all about music," she explained. "He lived it. That's all he thought about. And that was pretty much his life, that label and his artists."

He was, she found out, not the sort of guy who often let things roll off his back. And he cultivated his privacy. "He wasn't a very jolly man. He was very serious most of the time, very intimidating. Didn't say a lot, but when he did, you'd better listen to what he said! Because it usually was very smart.

"And he was very eccentric, like most super-smart artistic people."

Although she spoke with Gernhard on the phone every day, often Lynn wouldn't see him for a week or more. "I would drop CDs in his mailbox," she said, "and when he needed me to pick something up, he would leave it out front for me."

One Thanksgiving, she recalled, she called Gernhard and "begged" him to join her and her family for Thanksgiving dinner at her mom's house, "because he didn't have anybody to spend it with." He didn't show.

Over time, however, Gernhard came to depend on her. They'd meet at the Waffle House in Brentwood and discuss their plans for whatever artist they were working on, over scrambled eggs and hash browns.

A single mother, Lynn wanted to enroll her young son in Christ Presbyterian Academy, but she couldn't afford the tuition.

Gernhard — still the chivalrous white knight - paid for it himself.

"He was so good to my family," Lynn said. "Phil would send us Christmas cookie jars, just great stuff. He was always so nice. It was through the label that I got my bonus, but I feel like Phil — since he was the only person I knew — had put in a good word for me."

She only met Mike Curb after she'd worked for his company for several years.

Lynn spoke with the heavily-accented Mrs. Gernhard just once and briefly, during a Christmas get-together at the Gallimore home. It was awkward, but by then she had learned not to ask personal questions of Phil. "It was not unlike him to be very private, very 'Stay out of my business — if I want you to know, I'll tell you.'

"He could also be very harsh at times — but looking back, it was good for me. If you can work for Phil Gernhard, you're doing good. I enjoyed working for him because I learned a lot about music."

The label had faith in Rodney Atkins, but he'd failed to make much of an impact since he'd joined the roster — so much so that his Curb handlers convinced him to make a 180-degree change in musical approach, record producer and even physical appearance (his cowboy hat was traded in for a "workingman"-type ball cap), and try things again.

His first album as the "new Rodney," 2003's *Honesty*, produced a Top Ten hit in the title track, but no others that registered.

There wasn't much enthusiasm in the air as Atkins cut tracks for a followup. "We'd spent a half-million dollars of Mike Curb's money and had nothing to show for it," Atkins explained. "Never released the album."

After a heart-to-heart with Curb himself, "That's when Phil came in. And everything changed. Who I was, my confidence ... it was OK that I didn't want to record what was on the radio at the time."

Rodney Atkins' success became a personal mission. As he'd done 10 years earlier with Tim McGraw, Gernhard helped choose the songs that would be released as singles, aimed them at specific radio markets, and oversaw nearly every aspect of the fledgling performer's career.

"Phil wasn't an A&R guy," Atkins said, "he was THE guy. He wasn't your normal go-find-songs guy. Phil worked in the promotion staff, he had been a producer ... I kept saying 'Why don't you come in and produce this stuff with us?' He said "Naw, I got bad habits when I was in the studio. I'll work every inch of this that I can. I just can't go in the studio.'"

Gernhard instructed Atkins to "forget everything that had come before" when he went back into the studio with producer Ted Hewitt. We're starting over, he announced. "He said 'forget those producers, they're just tainting what your vision is. They're making it about them, and it can't be that. I'm telling everybody to leave you alone. I'm going to teach you how to find your own voice. How to produce your own records. How to be tough on yourself.' Man, we talked every week at least, sometimes more. He was the biggest music mentor I've ever had."

Under Gernhard's watchful eye, Atkins re-invented himself as a songwriter ... and a singer. "I'd sung live a lot, in the corner of a bar, playing for tips with a real shitty sound system, or no sound system," Atkins said. "I didn't know how to sing on a microphone. He explained to me about actors: 'Somebody that's on Broadway, they have to do big movements, move their hands to send emotions out, move their body in big ways. Some people can't make the transition to a camera because it's so sensitive it picks up just raising an eyebrow.'

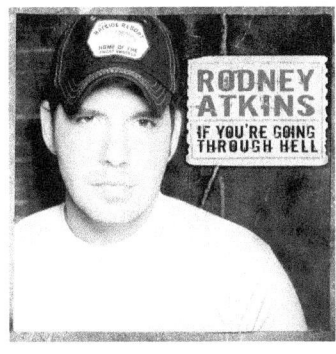

"He said 'You're behind the camera now. The microphone is so sensitive, you have to learn that you don't have to work quite as hard.' And that was eye-opening. Or ear-opening! He encouraged me to forget the rules, forget everything I'd heard or been told and just figure it out. So I started working at home."

The first song recorded for Atkins' second Curb album was a hardscrabble country rocker, "If You're Going Through Hell." Atkins and Hewitt proudly played the finished cut for Gernhard's approval.

"We turned the song into Phil and he said 'I like this, I like your vocal. I need you guys to go put bagpipes on it.'"

Bagpipes.

"And we're going 'This guy's crazy! He's fuckin' crazy!'"

Still, Atkins continued, "We went in and put bagpipes on it ... and it really became an anthem. It's crazy. It changed that record and gave it an almost church feel."

The album, similarly titled *If You're Going Through Hell*, was released late in 2006. "When we finished the album, he called me and said 'Congratulations. You've got an album that's gonna change your life."

Rodney Atkins, who knew this album was probably going to be his last shot at the brass ring, watched the first three singles, one after the other, make No. 1 — "If You're Going Through Hell," "Watching You" and "These Are My People."

It changed his life.

It was Kelly Lynn who "discovered" 16-year-old singer Ashley Gearing, during a performance at the Bluebird Café, the Nashville "listening room" where songwriters traditionally went to try out new material on audiences made up of mostly industry people. The Bluebird was the country music equivalent of Schwab's Drugstore in Los Angeles — you went there in hopes of getting noticed.

Gearing had scored a minor hit at the age of 12, "Can You Hear Me When I Talk to You," on the Disney-owned label Lyric Street. The Massachusetts native became the youngest singer to enter *Billboard*'s country singles chart, breaking the record set by Brenda Lee in the 1950s.

When Kelly Lynn heard her at the Bluebird, Gearing was on the market again.

Immediately, Kelly brought her to Phil Gernhard. "We sat down and within the first 10 minutes he said he wanted to sign me to Curb Records," Gearing recalled. "He said 'With a voice like yours, I want you to work with Byron Gallimore and no other. Because he's the best.' He was very particular about how he wanted to do it."

Ashley Gearing became Gernhard's latest professional cause. "Phil was very protective of me. He really kept me close to his chest, and didn't want to show his cards to anyone else at Curb.

"Mike Curb was initially opposed to signing me, because he was nervous about how young I was. And he had just gone through a little bit of drama with LeAnn Rimes, and her family getting involved. He said he didn't want to sign another minor. And Phil said 'I don't care. I'll put up my own money and sign her.'

"Mike said 'Well, if you're that passionate about it, you have my support.'"

And so her sessions began, with Gallimore in the producer's chair. Gernhard was there, every single time. "In all the years we worked together," said Gallimore, "and I don't know if he just respected what we were doing, he never was like 'This track isn't right; you need to go back and fix it.' He never did that to us. It was never like he was trying to produce from his side of the desk.

"I guess he just trusted me, I don't know. He never beat us up. And I'm sure there was plenty he could've said!"

He didn't interrupt while tape was running, but he had plenty to say afterwards, while the recorded tracks were being evaluated. "And," said Gearing, "Byron listened."

Gearing said she got the impression that her record was a "passion project" for Gernhard. He was, for example, extremely particular about the songs Gallimore had her cutting. He had a vision for her. He was meticulous about the lyrics.

"I knew he'd had a lot of pain in his lifetime," Gearing noted, "and sometimes Byron would have to say 'Phil! She's 16 years old, we can't have her singing all of these painful songs!' Phil said 'But I want to hear them from her perspective. She can act them out.'

"He'd say that he wanted me to be marketed one way, but then he'd find another sad song he wanted me to sing."

It was Gernhard, she said, who insisted she complete high school in her Massachusetts hometown, with her friends, and not move to Nashville until she'd graduated. Then she could finish her education at Belmont University. He was adamant she not give herself over too soon to the music industry.

At Curb headquarters, by way of introduction, Gearing and Gallimore performed a short acoustic showcase for the label staff. Afterwards, Mike Curb — whom she had yet to meet — approached her.

"You're bringing Phil Gernhard back to life," he said. "With this project, I've never seen him so happy, so excited, so passionate. This is the old Phil. This is my old friend."

It was 2007. "I know he had a lot of doctor's appointments," Lynn said. "I brought him muffins and left them on the front door because there were times he didn't have anybody, and he couldn't even get out to get groceries.

"There was a day I called and said 'There's a song I have just got to bring to the house,' and he just wasn't in the mood. I think he must have had some bad news. But he never would divulge it to me." Gearing watched him struggle to lift his frail body up into the cab of his big Humvee and wondered about his health. "He looked emaciated," recalled Curb, "but he functioned so beautifully."

Judee Gernhard said her brother had called her house in California and confessed: He'd been diagnosed with prostate cancer. And, typically, he didn't want anyone else to know.

"Phil would call me, or my daughter in Texas, and he'd have us doing all this research on California oncology places," she said. "We'd talk for hours on the phone, and all of a sudden he would just drop off, and I wouldn't know anything for weeks and months.

"He was self-medicating, and he got into lots of weird drugs and herbs — we found that when we cleaned out the house after he died."

Gernhard told her he was hoping to avoid surgery, because he feared it would leave him impotent.

It was around this same time, according to Judee, that her brother called with more devastating news. He'd Googled his absentee wife's name, and followed it down each and every rabbit hole, until he found her website:

She was also known as "Madeline Hamilton," a Stockholm-based escort whose services cost the equivalent of $750 per hour. The site was filled with salacious photographs of Mrs. Gernhard, and descriptions of just what the purchaser would receive for his "donation." She often traveled to the United States, it said, and could be "booked" for extended visits.

"He was devastated," said Judee. "He felt stupid, and he felt vulnerable. And this was right around the time he found out he had prostate cancer."

Gernhard was intensely private, but he was also a manipulator - and an accomplished liar.

Was he devastated? Did he know that Anna Maria Madeline Bosdotter Pettersson Gernhard was more than just the flirtatious makeup girl he met during a video shoot? Did he run off to Vegas and get married anyway?

"I'll bet he did know," Lynn said. "I'll bet he didn't care. He wasn't a judgmental person. He was very eccentric. He had pictures of naked women all over his house. I went into Phil's house a few times, they weren't photos, they were beautiful portraits, oil paintings of gorgeous, beautiful women.

"That's why I say that - I don't think he was very conservative. He was not 'my southern Baptist preacher brother.'"

June 2007: Gernhard and Curb with 16-year-old singer Ashley Gearing, just after her acoustic performance with Byron Gallimore for the Curb Records staff. From the collection of Ashley Gearing.

Ashley Gearing dropped by with Kelly, once. The paintings, she recalled, "weren't distasteful; I think he just really, truly appreciated the female body. Some people might think of all those naked pictures as sexual or creepy, but I think it was a deeper thing for him. An appreciation."

Gearing described the façade of Gernhard's home as "the kind place a family of five would live," a beautiful brick house in a nice, upscale suburban neighborhood.

Inside, it was a different story. "So dark, almost gothic," she said, "like a dark museum." There were no gold or platinum records on the walls downstairs, only the naked ladies, fixed and staring, and Gernhard's mounted collection of Samurai swords. "I don't think anybody ever visited him," Gearing said.

She and Kelly were there, at the boss' invitation, to view Elvis Presley's 1968 *Comeback Special* on DVD. They watched the entire 60-minute program in Gernhard's living room.

He was beaming, Gearing recalled. "He said 'This is the best show you'll ever see. This is what you're capable of. This is why I signed you.' He told Gearing she had Elvis-level stage presence, and after the show went online and bought — with her looking over his shoulder - a $200 pair of skinny jeans from Barney's. "He liked that I was tall and said I should always wear pants and heels," she said.

After a long day's work on her album, Gearing, Lynn, Gallimore and their families took Gernhard out for a celebratory dinner at a Japanese steakhouse. When the hibachi chef produced a sudden wall of flame from his skillet — part of the traditional tableside "performance" — Gernhard shrieked and recoiled in horror.

"I was sitting next to Phil, and he grabbed my arm like a little kid, and hid behind me," Gearing recalled. "He was mortified. We had to escort him out of the room for a second so he could catch his breath."

She and Lynn talked about it afterwards. Was there a bad fire experience buried deep in Phil's past? Had he been burned in more ways than one?

They never dared ask him about it. But they were stunned.

From there, events began to pick up speed, faster and faster, spiraling toward a terrible and inevitable conclusion.

Gernhard hired the private investigator to locate Betty Vernon, his high school sweetheart, in Florida. Once this was accomplished, he changed his will — "to keep it away from the hooker," in the words of his sister.

If my friend, Elizabeth Vernon, of Bradenton, Florida, survives me, I give my residuary estate, including any royalties to which my estate or I may be entitled, to the Trustee of the Philip A. Gernhard Trust (hereinafter referred to as the "Trust") described in Article B hereof.

Under "Provisions for Trust":

The Trustee shall distribute to or for the benefit of Elizabeth Vernon so much of the net income and principal as determined advisable for her health, maintenance, and support in reasonable comfort, as well as for the education, whether public, private or special, of the following named grandchildren and great grandchildren of Elizabeth Vernon ...

Gernhard signed this version of his Last Will and Testament on July 13, 2007, naming as executor his longtime accountant, Stephen Parker.

Five days later, he filed for divorce from Maria. In addition to the standard "Irreconcilable Differences," he listed his reasons for seeking termination of the marriage:

Wife has committed inappropriate marital conduct that would entitle Husband to a divorce.

Wife has willfully deserted and/or abandoned Husband, without reasonable cause, for one (1) whole year.

Wife has refused to come to Tennessee, without reasonable cause, and has been willfully absent from Husband for two (2) years.

The document also requested that "proper process issue and be served upon the Wife requiring her to answer this Complaint," and that the court make "an equitable division of the marital property between the parties."

Madeline Hamilton, from her website.

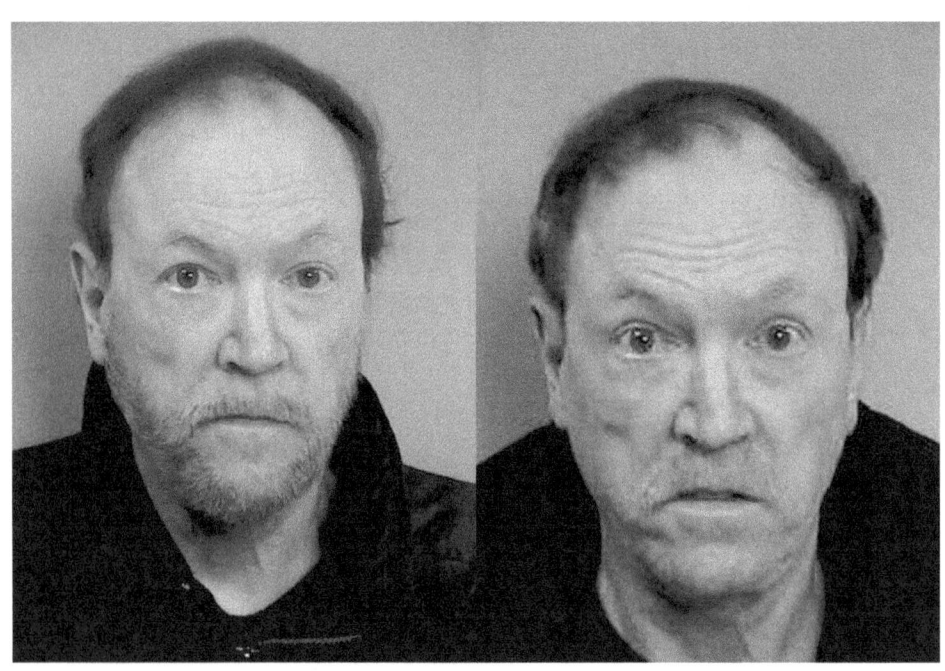

Dec. 31, 2007. Mugshots. Gernhard was arrested and booked for DUI on New Year's Eve. These are the last known photographs of him. Nashville Metro Police.

15

A Safe Place

"These Are My People," the third single from *If You're Going Through Hell*, reached No. 1 in September 2007. It was cause for great celebration — three chart-toppers in a row! — but Gernhard, who was eager to turn his attention away from private matters, wasn't finished working the Rodney Atkins album.

He pushed for a fourth single, and on Oct. 1, "Cleaning This Gun (Come on in Boy)" was released. "A lot of people at the label at the time thought it was too risky, because it was about kids and guns," Atkins said. "But I'd been playing it out in the real world, and so Phil and I talked about it. He asked me about some of the responses I got. Then he went after it with radio, testing the waters and stuff."

Six years earlier, Tim McGraw's *Set This Circus Down* album had spawned four consecutive Number Ones. With the Atkins project, Gernhard was hoping to repeat that near-impossible feat.

Mike Curb: "Phil was saying to me 'Oh, if I could just get one more No. 1 with Rodney, I will have duplicated what we did with Tim — and maybe that will cause Tim to realize the role that I played.'

"I said 'Phil, it doesn't matter! I mean, Tim knows the role you played. But artists are never going to come up and say 'What would we have done without you?'"

As Gernhard and the Curb promotion team were working to turn "Cleaning This Gun" into a hit, Betty Vernon invited her long-lost friend to Bradenton, to spend Thanksgiving with her extended family.

When he returned to Nashville, he was almost a different man.

"We were having lunch one day," Curb said. "I remember sitting in our dining room, and Phil started talking about a 'safe place' he had found.

"He told us about a lady in Florida that he had dated back in high school, 'but her parents didn't want me around, so I had to leave, and she married someone else.'

"He said 'Then I was searching through numerous girlfriends, and four marriages, for that safe place. And I have now found it.'"

As the divorce dragged on into 2008, Phil continued to throw himself into his work, overseeing the Ashley Gearing project with Byron Gallimore, and engineering a clear road at radio for "Cleaning This Gun," about which he was supremely confident. It could be done.

Through their lawyers, he and Maria finally agreed on terms for their divorce. The alimony settlement was generous. The papers were in Stockholm, in her hands; once she signed and returned them, it would all be over.

As was his custom, Gernhard spent Christmas Day with Mike and Linda Curb at their palatial home outside of Nashville. He seemed, Curb thought, considerably steadier than he had in a long time. His eyes, though still dark and distant, held their gaze.

On New Year's Eve, Metro Police stopped the Humvee on Tennessee's Interstate 440, near the Nashville city limits. According to the report, the big black car was swerving across traffic lanes; Gernhard's eyes were dilated, and his speech slurred, and admitted to taking three Valiums.

He was arrested and booked for DUI. His mugshots show a disheveled man with suspicious eyes and a four-day beard, glaring into the camera shell-shocked, royally pissed off and backed defensively into a corner.

Phil didn't let just anyone see into the windows of his soul. "The one thing that bothered me was that I could never really see his eyes," Gearing said. "He wore dark sunglasses that weren't black, but kind of brownish ... I'm the kind of person who connects with people by looking in their eyes, and you never could because he always had his glasses on. And the few times that I did see his eyes, it was kind of alarming because I realized how much pain was in them.

"A few times in the studio, he would take them off and put his hands over his face, and really listen to the music, really get into it. And that made me happy, because I felt like he took his glasses off, he was letting his guard down a little bit."

The Gernhard-engineered plan was to release an Ashley Gearing single to radio in the spring and see how it performed. If "Out the Window" was a hit, they'd drop a second single and follow that with the full album.

In the meantime, "Cleaning This Gun" climbed the chart through January and into February.

April 2007: Gernhard, left, and Mike Curb congratulate Rodney Atkins on the success of his second consecutive No. 1, "Watching You." Curb Records.

Monday, Feb. 18, 2008 was Presidents' Day, a national holiday. The Curbs were in Florida for the annual auto races at Daytona.

Mike Curb: "Phil was always the guy who called me and said 'Guess what — I just found out we're going to be No. 1 tomorrow.' But this was a holiday, and he couldn't download *Billboard*. He'd left me a message saying 'I can't figure out where we are; did we make it with Rodney?' Meaning did we make it to No. 1?'

"One of our employees knew a man at *Billboard*, and he called to say 'Incredible news — I just found out we're going to be No. 1 when *Billboard* goes to print!'

"I picked up the phone and called Phil. "Phil — congratulations! I just got word that 'Cleaning This Gun' is going to be No. 1!' He said "'Oh my God. That's so good.' He said 'Wow, I needed this.' Saying things that, when you look back at it, he was saying 'OK. I've done it.'

"You can't imagine how many times I've tried to re-create, in my mind, what we talked about that last time."

Phil called Rodney Atkins to tell him the good news. Atkins remembers every word of their conversation. "He told me he was proud of me. He told me to make sure I keep writing. He said if you don't stay creative, you get sick. And he actually told me he loved me."

Which he'd never done before. "That was the last time I talked to him."

On Tuesday morning, Phil and Kelly met on schedule at the Waffle House. They were ostensibly there to discuss Atkins, and his incredible quartet of chart-toppers. But the meeting was anything but celebratory.

"He didn't even really want to talk music that day," said Lynn. "He wasn't too interested in my CD. And that was very weird. That's why he hired me — that's all I did. That was our only reason to connect, was to give him my songs." They exchanged congratulations, but something, Lynn perceived, was definitely "off" about her boss. He seemed even more distant than usual.

"I told him 'Byron's been trying to get in touch with you.' He pretty much had cut most of us off.

"He paid for the little Waffle House breakfast, and it was pretty much 'See ya later, bye.'"

He slowly pulled himself up into the big black Hummer, closed the door and drove off.

Bill DeYoung | 183

By Friday, the 22nd, he hadn't returned calls, from anyone. Which was unusual. The telephone was Phil's mainline.

At lunchtime, Kelly drove over to the Brentwood house. She rang the bell, and pounded on the front door, but there was no response from inside. "So I called Mike's secretary and I said 'I feel like I've got to go check on Phil. I beat on the door, and he's not answering.'

"She said 'Don't go in. Let me handle it.'"

Secretary Becky Judd contacted another Curb employee, a man who knew Phil, to go and check on him, too. Again, there was no response, and the police were summoned.

"I went to my son's school, which was about four miles down the road," Lynn said. "And I had a really bad feeling. It had been like four days and I had not talked to him, which was not normal. At all. Because he would at least call back and say 'I'm not going to go to work, I don't feel good,' or whatever, but he would never not just get in touch with me. I was pretty much the only point of contact, I think, at that time."

Just before 1 p.m., after their entreaties met only silence, officers broke a side window and entered the dark, silent house. They found Phil Gernhard on the floor of his bedroom, the back of his head blown out. A silver revolver was found next to the body.

"I'll never forget the minute I walked out of my son's school I got a call saying that he was gone," Lynn recalled. "And I literally fell to my knees in the school parking lot. It was the worst news I'd ever gotten in my life.

"And also, I felt responsible. Any time somebody takes their life, you want to say why? Are you kidding me? I need you here, we've got stuff to do, we've got an artist to break.

"What happened? And what could I have done?"

Missi Gallimore arrived, and together they sat in her car, in Phil's driveway, and sobbed.

"If you look at the pad of paper he had in front of him when he died, he had a list of 14 things," said Curb. "He had just completed the album with Ashley Gearing. He had the CD on his desk. And there was a note about Rodney.

"It was almost like 'Life is complete. No more pain. No more heartbreak. No more being sued by women.' It was like 'My life is complete, I've done the best I can do, I've achieved what I want to achieve. I'm ready to go.' That was the gist of it.

"It wasn't a suicide note. It wasn't a goodbye note. It was just a note of completion that tied right into the safe place. He'd found the safe place. A lot of people call that God, or they call it heaven, but he called it a safe place."

It was, Curb also noted, almost exactly 50 years since Gernhard had made his very first records, as a college student in South Carolina. Was the circle complete?

Because the circumstances of his death ("perforating intra-oral gunshot wound") indicated suicide, the medical examiner did not check Gernhard's body for cancer — although the autopsy report noted that the decedent's prostate was "unusually enlarged and nodular" — nor was a test conducted that would reveal the presence of drugs used to treat the disease.

Noted, however, was the presence of the opiate painkiller Darvocet (a combination of propoxyphene and acetaminophen). Within two years, the FDA would recommend that Darvocet no longer be used, due to potential cardiac-related side effects.

One by one, the calls were made: To Sandy in Florida, Judee in California, Deborah in North Carolina. To Dick Holler and Johnny McCullough, Kent LaVoie and Jim Stafford and the Royal Guardsmen. Kelly called Ashley Gearing at her family's home in Massachusetts.

"The thing that beat me up about it," reflected Rodney Atkins, "was that I don't feel like I told him enough how much he meant to me. I don't know if that would've changed his mind or not about what he did.

"You assume a guy like that is a rock, because he was that hard-ass drill sergeant kind of guy. And you thought he could muscle through anything. We didn't even realize he was crumbling like that."

Steve Parker, Phil's executor, told Betty Vernon that her high school suitor had indeed left everything to her — not his sister, not any of his ex-wives. Not Kelly Lynn, not his friends from Curb or anywhere else. Just her.

But the will was being contested, Parker told her, by Gernhard's fourth and last spouse. The divorce was not yet final; Maria hadn't signed the

papers. It might take months — it might take years — for Vernon to realize anything, including the trust fund Gernhard had sought to create
for her grandchildren and great-grandchildren.

In the meantime, the Vernons were free to go on the Alaskan cruise,
which Phil had paid for before his suicide. He'd killed himself before
signing a check for the scenic drive down the Pacific Coast Highway, so
that part of the promise was off.

They went ahead and took the cruise, drinking many toasts to their
departed benefactor, and flew home at their own expense.

Privately, Betty had a lot to think about.

Ashley Gearing's single
"Out the Window" was released
in March. "At that point, I
didn't know anybody at Curb,"
she said. "I knew Kelly, I knew
Phil — and that was all I needed, because Phil could sign off
on anything.

"But Phil wasn't ready to
release me to the world. He
was very strategic about that.
That's why, when I got the call,
I was like ... the book isn't finished." But Curb called her in
to the big office and said, som-
berly, they were going to put the record out ... "for Phil."

"Out the Window" was not a success, although a followup single performed marginally better. In the end, however, Curb Records never released Gearing's album. She left the label to try again somewhere else.

The September 18 edition of *Nashville Scene*, a local alt-weekly newspaper religiously devoured by the music community, revealed in its
cover story ("Number One With a Bullet") the lurid details of Gernhard's
final years and suicide.

The reporter ferreted out a deposition given by the widow Gernhard
shortly after Phil had filed for divorce, accusing her of "improper marital
conduct," the previous July.

"I provided sex under a legal escort service with several men," she was quoted as saying. "But not several men at the same time. There were no romantic relationships with any other men. My husband supported my legal escort business."

Maria also claimed that Gernhard knew she was an escort when he married her, and that she had her "husband's approval, support and encouragement."

Maria sold the Brentwood house in 2009, for just under a half-million dollars.

No one will ever know what was going on in Phil Gernhard's mind. He left no letter, no diary, no way to know for certain what was true and what was false and what drove him to take his own life. And because he had no close friends, it isn't likely that somebody will come forward and explain everything the way Phil might have wanted it explained.

Throughout his life and career, he told different stories to different people. The absolute truth of *who* he was will always be a mystery.

We do, however, know *what* Phil Gernhard was — an inordinately talented man who left us with a vast catalog of recorded music, some of it absolutely brilliant, some not so much, but all of it bearing the indelible mark of Phillip Arnold Gernhard.

He changed a lot of lives on his journey. Kent LaVoie, who owes his current state of financial comfort and stability to Phil Gernhard, often imagines the conversation he and his old friend might have had.

"What I wish I'd said to him was: 'Phil, I'm not here for anything. I just want to thank you. I'm fat because of you. Thanks.' I felt bad about not doing that, because I had plenty of opportunities.

"If he hadn't come up to me that day, I would never have been in this business. I would probably be playing on Clearwater Beach at 70, with some 40-year-old chick, half-loaded and just having a good time."

Acknowledgements

Thanks to Michelle Allen, Larry Applebaum, Dominic Carini, Steve Cavendish, Joshua Clark, Dennis Coffey, Cheri L. Cranford, Phyllis Crosby, Johnny Dark, Cherie Diez, Homer Fesperman, Artie Fletcher, Morgan Frankel, Bob Frost, Caesar Gallegos and the Charles M. Schulz Museum, Tom Gribbin, Joanne Heiland, David Holler, Richard Hunt, Sian Hunter, Steve Huntington, Frank Jakes, Raette Johnson, Becky Judd, Robert Lipartito, Jane Mandelbaum, Ron Maniscalo, John McCutcheon, Bill McGill, Wendy McKay, William McKeen, Trent Notestine, Steven Parker, Samuel Perryman, Bob Ross, Tim Rozgonyi, Dave Schlenker, Rick Schmidt, Rick Simmons, PJ Tobia, Ed Tucker, Harry Turner, Wes Vause, John Veciana, Jim Vernon, Cyril Vetter, Patty Ware, April Weatherly, Emily West, Gary White, Maurice Williams, James Wintle, Steve Zaritsky, Walter Zvonchenko.

And - always - to Amy Kagan.

The following were contacted and declined to be interviewed for this project: Dion DiMucci, Tony Scotti, David Bellamy, Howard Bellamy, Michael Lloyd, Doug Morris, Tim McGraw, Jo Dee Messina, Anna Maria Madeline Bosdotter Pettersson Gernhard.

Chart information was obtained from *"The Billboard Book of Top 40 Hits 1955-2000"* and *"Top Pop Albums 1955-1992,"* by Joel Whitburn (Billboard Books).

Lyrics to "Snoopy vs. the Red Baron" reprinted by permission of Dick Holler, David Holler and Steven Parker, administrator of SanPhil Music Publishing.

Rest in Peace: Judee Gernhard, Deborah Triplett, Leo Gallagher, Jim Vernon.

Sources

Chapter 1: Rosebud

The ghost of a man standing in ... Author interview with Betty Vernon, Oct. 2, 2016, and numerous followups.

"brought him tremendous closure ..." "Number One With a Bullet" by P.J. Tobia, *Nashville Scene*, Sept. 18, 2008.

Additional details in this chapter were verified by Sandy Gernhard, Judee Gernhard, Kelly Lynn, Mike Curb and Dick Holler.

Chapter 2: All Shook Up

In Boyd Rains Gernhard's mind, there were two ways ... Author interview with Judee Gernhard, Oct. 13, 2016.

She confessed that she'd never ... Author interview with Sandy Gernhard, Oct. 17, 2016.

America's entry into World War II ... Boyd R. "Bud" Gernhard's self-authored obituary, undated.

"You couldn't get metal parts or rubber during the war ..." Author interview with Judee Gernhard, Oct. 13, 2016.

And he got involved in the community ... Boyd R. "Bud" Gernhard's self-authored obituary, undated.

Midwestern circus king John Ringling ... "Biography of John and Mable Ringing," www.ringling.org.

When Judee and Phil Gernhard were growing up ... Author interview with Betty Vernon, Oct. 2, 2016; Author interview with Judee Gernhard, Oct. 13, 2016; Author interview with Dick Thieland, Oct. 16, 2016.

The Gernhards lived in several different homes ... *Author interview with Judee Gernhard, Oct. 13, 2016.*

"He was out on the road a lot ..." Author interview with Judee Gernhard, Nov. 11, 2016.

Phil's buddy George Heiland saw up close ... Author interview with George Heiland, Oct. 16, 2016.

"We were part of the same neighborhood ..." Author interview with Betty Vernon, Oct. 2, 2016, and followups.

"Phil was kind of quiet and introspective ..." Author interview with Sandy Gernhard, Oct. 10, 2016.

While 8-year-old Phil was away at Camp St. Andrew ... "Covering Sarasota With the Main Street Reporter," *Sarasota Herald-Tribune,* July 17, 1949.

"In junior high and high school, he was not ..." Author interview with Judee Gernhard, Nov. 11, 2016.

Betty Van Doninck attended one of them ... Author interview with Betty Vernon, Oct. 2, 2016, and followups.

"That night had a tremendous impact on my life ..." "Music Man: Phil Gernhard Has Ear For Music and Eye For the Right Artist," *Sarasota Herald-Tribune,* Sept. 3, 1988.

"Phil never aspired to be in the military ..." *Author interview with Judee Gernhard, Oct. 13, 2016.*

In his senior year at Sarasota High School ... "Interested in Naval ROTC," *Sarasota Herald-Tribune* 1957 (exact date unknown); "With the Services," *Sarasota News,* June 25, 1958.

"He loved being in South Carolina ..." Author interview with Judee Gernhard, Nov. 11, 2016.

Chapter 3: Oh Won't You Stay

"I heard people talking about production ..." Author interview with Johnny McCullough, Oct. 18, 2016.

Born and raised in South Carolina, Maurice Williams ... "Maurice Williams' Lifetime of Beautiful Melodies," *Goldmine*, April 6, 2011; Maurice Williams biography, allmusic.com.

After a summer '59 show in Columbia ... Author interview with Judee Gernhard, Oct. 13, 2016; "Music Man: Phil Gernhard Has Ear For Music and Eye For the Right Artist," *Sarasota Herald-Tribune*, Sept. 3, 1988.

"He found out I was a producer and he wanted ..." Author interview with Johnny McCullough, Oct. 18, 2016.

They named their company Briarwood Enterprises, after the ... Author interview with Dick Holler, Oct. 3, 2016; Author interview with Johnny McCullough, Oct. 18, 2016.

The only thing that could even pass for a recording studio ... abccolumbia.com/about-us/history; Author interview with Johnny McCullough, Oct. 18, 2016; "My First Recording as an Artist," DennisCoffeySite.com, April 25, 2015; "A Boomer's Memories" by Rick Wrigley, May 19, 2013, aboomersmemories.com; Author interview with Dick Holler, Oct. 3, 2016.

Sometime late in the summer of 1960 ... The Billboard Book of Number One Hits, Fred Bronson, Billboard Publications.

"One mistake, and we went back to the top ..." Author interview with Johnny McCullough, Oct. 18, 2016.

Gernhard always told a slightly different version ... The Billboard Book of Number One Hits, Fred Bronson, Billboard Publications.

When he said to sing it flat ... *Setting the Record Straight, Vol. 2: The Music and Careers of Recording Artists From the 1950s and Early '60s in Their Own Words by Anthony P. Musso, AuthorHouse.*

"I went back up there, and Silver started playin' the new tape." Author interview with Johnny McCullough, Oct. 18, 2016.

Not long after "Stay" became a smash ... Author interview with Dick Holler, Oct. 3, 2016.

They "discovered" Columbia-area R&B vocalist Thelma Bynum ... email exchange with Quia Thompson, April 5, 2024.

In the middle of all the Briarwood excitement, Gernhard ... Author interview with Dick Holler, Oct. 3, 2016; Author interview with Judee Gernhard, Oct. 13, 2016.

He brought a pretty, dark-haired girl home to Sarasota ... Author interview with Judee Gernhard, Oct. 13, 2016.

"We were trying to make hit records ..." Author interview with Johnny McCullough, Oct. 18, 2016.

Briarwood Enterprises breathed no more. Author interview with Dick Holler, Oct. 3, 2016.

"He'd gotten off track ..." Author interview with Judee Gernhard, Oct. 13, 2016.

Boyd Gernhard was just finishing up ..."Boyd Gernhard Enters Clerk of Court Race," *Sarasota Journal*, Jan. 2, 1964.

"Boyd Gernhard to File for Circuit Court Clerk," *Venice Gondolier*, Jan. 6, 1964.

Chapter 4: I Want More

"I decided to go to Tampa for the old three-year law program ..." "The Middleman," the *Muezzin*, University of Tampa Alumni Magazine, May 1971.

Almost as soon as he started attending pre-law classes ... Author interview with Sandy Gernhard, Oct. 10, 2016.

"It's been a long time since I have believed ..." From the letters of Sandy Gernhard.

"Mom Gernhard was the one who really controlled the ship ..." Author interview with Sandy Gernhard, Oct. 10, 2016.

Nevertheless, Bud and his son had raised the white flag ... Author interview with Judee Gernhard, Oct. 13, 2016.

"I entered Tampa with the same arch-conservative ideas ..." the Muezzin, University of Tampa Alumni Magazine, May 1971.

He made the Honor Roll at UT ... Undated clippings from the *Sarasota Herald-Tribune* found in the Gernhard family scrapbook, confirmed by Sandy Gernhard.

"He wanted to be Clarence Darrow ..." Author interview with Sandy Gernhard, Oct. 10, 2016.

In July 1964, Dick and Marge Sexton ... "A Real Night Club — For Teens," *St. Petersburg Evening Independent*, Aug. 22, 1964.

With members from both sides of Tampa Bay ... Author email exchange with Charlie Souza, Oct. 15, 2016; Curtis, Kurt "K.O.T.O," *Florida's Famous & Forgotten: History of Florida's Rock, Soul & Dance Music, The First 30 Years 1955-1985, Florida Media, Inc.; Author interview with Marjorie Sexton, Oct. 7, 2016.*

Gernhard, meanwhile, was 24 years old and hungry ... Author interview with Sandy Gernhard, Oct. 10, 2016.

"Phil was a record producer, but he was out of work ..." Author interview with Marjorie Sexton, Oct. 7, 2016.

The Sarasota teen club was only open on weekends ... Author interview with Sandy Gernhard, Oct. 10, 2016.

Whenever some national act with a fresh hit ..." Author interview with Marjorie Sexton, Oct. 7, 2016.

"Phil was hustling and trying to get it done ..." Author interview with Kent LaVoie, Nov. 22, 2016.

He took the band into H&H Productions ... Author email exchange with Charlie Souza, Oct. 15, 2016; Author interview with Kent LaVoie, Nov. 22, 2016.

"The way it worked out ..." Author interview with Kent LaVoie, Nov. 22, 2016.

The Beats record is selling better ... From the letters of Sandy Gernhard.

"Everybody did it, but no record was played as much ..." Author interview with Kent LaVoie, Nov. 22, 2016.

At the urging of Marge Sexton ... Author interview with Marjorie Sexton, Oct. 7, 2016.

"Phil was an energetic, creative guy ..." Author email exchange with Charlie Souza, Oct. 15, 2016.

"She said 'We've got this great new connection ...'" Author interview with Ronny Elliott, Sept. 24, 2016, and followups.

Charles Fuller Hunt was a sound engineer ... Author interview with Ronny Elliott, Sept. 24, 2016, and email followups; Author interview with John Centinaro, Oct. 2, 2016; Author interview with studio manager Phyllis Crosby, Oct. 2, 2016; Curtis, Kurt "K.O.T.O," *Florida's Famous & Forgotten: History of Florida's Rock, Soul & Dance Music, The First 30 Years 1955-1985, Florida Media, Inc.*

By the time the Outsiders cut their third single ... Author interview with Ronny Elliott, Sept. 24, 2016, and followups.

"When we went in to record 'King Bee,' the Laurie people said ..." Author interview with Ronny Elliott, Sept. 24, 2016, and followups.

"His mother said 'He's chasing that pie in the sky ...'" Author interview with Sandy Gernhard, Oct. 10, 2016.

"Law school was a big disappointment ... "The Middleman," the *Muezzin*, University of Tampa Alumni Magazine, May 1971.

Chapter 5: In the Nick of Time, a Hero Arose

In October of 1965, cartoonist Charles M. Schulz ... Michaelis, David, *Schulz and Peanuts*, Harper Publishing.

"Can you think of a funnier name for an airplane?" Snoopy and the Red Baron Exhibition Celebrates 50th Anniversary of Snoopy as the World War I Flying Ace, Charles M. Schulz Museum press release, Oct. 6, 2015.

There had been actual Sopwith Camels ... *Manfred von Richthofen: The Red Baron, by Stephen Sherman, acepilots.com.*

... inspired by a model Fokker in his young son's room ... Michaelis, David, *Schulz and Peanuts*, Harper Publishing.

"*Peanuts* was one of Mom and Dad Gernhard's favorite ..." Author interview with Sandy Gernhard, Oct. 29, 2016.

This made Gernhard, sitting in one boring law seminar after another ... "The Middleman," the *Muezzin*, University of Tampa Alumni Magazine, May 1971.

Holler had been a huge fan of singer/songwriter Johnny Horton's ... Author interview with Dick Holler, Nov. 12, 2016.

"I had always been something of an aviation freak ..." Author interview with Dick Holler, Nov. 12, 2016.

Lyrics to "Snoopy vs. the Red Baron" by Dick Holler and Phil Gernhard, published by SanPhil Music. Used by permission.

"We had the whole thing cut ..." Author interview with Dick Holler, Nov. 12, 2016.

Phil and Sandy were married in Sarasota ... "Gernhard-Thompson Vows Said Saturday," *St. Petersburg Times*, Aug. 8, 1966.

"I took the basic Red Baron idea ..." "Sarasota Law Student a Show Biz Success: Snoopy and Royal Guardsmen to Hit Parade Peak," *Tampa Tribune*, Dec. 23, 1967.

"Phil brought the song here for us ..." Author interview with Ronny Elliott, Sept. 24, 2016.

Gernhard, undaunted, went back to the Surfer's Club ... Author email exchange with Charlie Souza, Oct. 15, 2016.

Gernhard then turned to the Royal Guardsmen ... "The Middleman," the *Muezzin*, University of Tampa Alumni Magazine, May 1971.

The Royal Guardsmen came from Ocala ... "Cross-Country Tour Ahead For Local 6-Member Musical Group," *Ocala Star-Banner*, Dec. 15, 1966.

Nunley (at 20, the oldest Guardsman) was studying business ... Author interview with Chris Nunley, Bill Balogh and Billy Taylor, Oct. 1, 2016.

"Although it gets noisy at times ..." "Cross-Country Tour Ahead For Local 6-Member Musical Group," Ocala Star-Banner, Dec. 15, 1966.

The Royal Guardsmen had been introduced ... Author interview with Chris Nunley, Bill Balogh and Billy Taylor, Oct. 1, 2016.

It was the only place in the city ... Author interview with John Centinaro, Oct. 2, 2016.

Veciana got the Ocala sextet a booking at the Spot ... Author interview with Chris Nunley, Bill Balogh and Billy Taylor, Oct. 1, 2016.

Gernhard, who had a handshake arrangement ... Author interview with John Centinaro, Oct. 2, 2016.

At their first Charles Fuller session ... Author interview with Chris Nunley, Bill Balogh and Billy Taylor, Oct. 1, 2016.

As the single was beginning its slow rise to nowhere ... Author interview with John Centinaro, Oct. 2, 2016.

"We were setting up our equipment, when Phil comes up ..." Author interview with Chris Nunley, Bill Balogh and Billy Taylor, Oct. 1, 2016.

"We were a bunch of pie-eyed kids ..." Author interview with Barry Winslow, Oct. 2, 2016.

"Gernhard came to town and we played the song for him ..." Author interview with Chris Nunley, Bill Balogh and Billy Taylor, Oct. 1, 2016.

"We were surprised ..." Author email exchange with John Burdett, Oct. 17, 2016, with followups.

With the underage Guardsmen's parents looking on ... "Sarasota Law Student a Show Biz Success: Snoopy and Royal Guardsmen to Hit Parade Peak," Tampa Tribune, Dec. 23, 1967.

"At first, they couldn't believe I was serious ..." "The Middleman," the 6-Member Musical Group," Ocala Star-Banner, University of Tampa Alumni Magazine, May 1971.

The song was cut quickly at Fuller ... Author interview with Chris Nunley, Bill Balogh and Billy Taylor, Oct. 1, 2016; Author interview with Barry Winslow, Oct. 2, 2016.

"Our little studio did not have any high end audio stuff ..." John "Zeke" Brumage on the amazon.com review page for the CD issue of *Snoopy vs. the Red Baron/Snoopy and His Friends*, dated Sept. 21, 2004.

Still, it needed something — a memorable kickoff! ... Author interview with Chris Nunley, Bill Balogh and Billy Taylor, Oct. 1, 2016.

In the middle section of the recording ... Only one copy of this version, pressed onto a 7-inch vinyl test pressing from Charles Fuller Hunt's company Omni Media, is known to exist. It is in the hands of collector and Royal Guardsmen uber-fan Ed Tucker.

"Phil told me that he showed the song ..." Author interview with Dick Holler, Oct. 3, 2016.

Bob and Gene Schwartz were shrewd enough ... "The Laurie Label Story," bsnpub.com, March 25, 2009.

"The lawyers said 'Here's what's gonna happen ...'" Author interview with Dick Holler, Oct. 3, 2016.

Gernhard wrote the cartoonist a personal letter ... Author interview with Dick Holler, Oct. 3, 2016; Author interview with Sandy Gernhard, Oct. 29, 2016.

But Schulz, as was his wont with such things ... Michaelis, David, *Schulz and Peanuts*, Harper Publishing.

Gernhard ordered Guardsmen Winslow and Nunley ... Author interview with Chris Nunley, Bill Balogh and Billy Taylor, Oct. 1, 2016.

"Laurie had a whole system of DJs ..." Author interview with Dick Holler, Oct. 3, 2016.

"Most records get airplay in all the minor areas first ..." Author interview with Barry Winslow, Oct. 2, 2016, and email followups.

"First time I remember hearing the song on the radio ..." Author interview with Chris Nunley, Bill Balogh and Billy Taylor, Oct. 1, 2016.

"He picked me up and sat me on the kitchen counter ..." Author interview with Sandy Gernhard, Oct. 10, 2016.

"Snoopy vs. the Red Baron" sold more than a million copies in its first week ... "The Royal Guardsmen's Snoopy Connection," *Goldmine*, Dec. 18, 2015.

Laurie Records had to sub-contract ... Author interview with Chris Nunley, Bill Balogh and Billy Taylor, Oct. 1, 2016.

"It was within a month's time frame, literally ..." Author interview with Barry Winslow, Oct. 2, 2016.

Dick Holler, who was working in a hardware store ... Author interview with Dick Holler, Oct. 6, 2016.

The story goes that Charles M. Schulz ... Michaelis, David, *Schulz and Peanuts*, Harper Publishing.

Gernhard pointed this out ... Author interview with Sandy Gernhard, Oct. 10, 2016.

In the end, according to Dick Holler ... Author interview with Dick Holler, Oct. 6, 2016.

The Royal Guardsmen's cut ... Author interview with Chris Nunley, Bill Balogh and Billy Taylor, Oct. 1, 2016.

High school students in 1966 were forbidden from ... Author interview with Chris Nunley, Bill Balogh and Billy Taylor, Oct. 1, 2016; Author interview with Barry Winslow, Oct. 2, 2016.

The Royal Guardsmen couldn't capitalize on their success ... Author interview with Chris Nunley, Bill Balogh and Billy Taylor, Oct. 1, 2016; Author email exchange with John Burdett, Oct. 17, 2016; "Cross-Country Tour Ahead For Local 6-Member Musical Group," *Ocala Star-Banner*, Dec. 15, 1966.

... it was knocked out over 21 sweaty hours at the Fuller studio ... Author interview with Chris Nunley, Bill Balogh and Billy Taylor, Oct. 1, 2016; Author interview with Billy Taylor, Oct. 31, 2016; Author email exchange with John Burdett, Oct. 17, 2016; John "Zeke" Brumage on the amazon.

com review page for the CD issue of *Snoopy vs. the Red Baron/Snoopy and His Friends*, dated Sept. 21, 2004.

"We were just given the songs and herded in there," Author interview with Billy Taylor, Oct. 31, 2016; "The Royal Guardsmen of Ocala on LP," *St. Petersburg Times*, Feb. 20, 1967.

"That first album cover was a disaster that Laurie came up with ..." Author interview with Dick Holler, Oct. 6, 2016.

"We'd go down to Phil's and work on business ... Author interview with Chris Nunley, Bill Balogh and Billy Taylor, Oct. 1, 2016.

"I knew it was going to be a good record the first time I heard it on radio ..." "'Snoopy' Scores a Hit," *St. Petersburg Times*, Jan. 15, 1967.

Chapter 6: Sopwith Camel Time

"I'd be one of the first done with the tracks..." Author interview with Chris Nunley, Bill Balogh and Billy Taylor, Oct. 1, 2016.

Because of the money he was raking in ... Author interview with Dick Holler, Oct. 6, 2016; "John Abbott Joins Laurie," *Billboard*, July 16, 1966.

"We were on a deadline ..." Author interview with Chris Nunley, Bill Balogh and Billy Taylor, Oct. 1, 2016.

Up in Andy Griffith's hometown ... Author interview with Dick Holler, Oct. 6, 2016. "A Law Student Forms 3-Fold Pop Complex," *Billboard*, March 25, 1967.

People were in and out of Gernhard Enterprises' rented bungalow ... Author interview with Ronny Elliott, Sept. 27, 2016; Author interview with Sandy Gernhard, Oct. 10, 2016; "Meet the Royal Guardsmen," *Hit Parader*, May 1967.

Local DJ Charles "Charlie Brown" Troxell was ... "A Law Student Forms 3-Fold Pop Complex," *Billboard*, March 25, 1967.

The boys let their guard down ... "The Royal Guardsmen: School-Going Guardsmen Still Spare-Time Hitsters," *New Musical Express*, March 25, 1967.

On May 3 Phil and Sandy ... BMI awards dinner program; Author interview with Sandy Gernhard, Oct. 10, 2016.

The youngest Guardsmen graduated from high school in June ... Author interview with Chris Nunley, Bill Balogh and Billy Taylor, Oct. 1, 2016.

Sam "Wooly Bully" Samudio was trying to shake ... Summer Shower of Stars your program; Sam the Sham biography, allmusic.com; Author interview with Chris Nunley, Bill Balogh and Billy Taylor, Oct. 1, 2016.

... the Royal Guardsmen, famous for their kiddie novelty songs ... Author interview with Chris Nunley, Bill Balogh and Billy Taylor, Oct. 1, 2016.

Their "entourage" consisted of Charles Troxell and Johnny McCullough ... Author interview with Johnny McCullough, Oct. 18, 2016.

"We were the openers on the tour ..." Author interview with Chris Nunley, Bill Balogh and Billy Taylor, Oct. 1, 2016.

The May 6 issue of *Billboard* included ... "Gernhard Office Opens in Texas," *Billboard*, May 6, 1967.

"We were pissed off at Gernhard and the record company ..." Author interview with Chris Nunley, Bill Balogh and Billy Taylor, Oct. 1, 2016.

"Snoopy's Christmas" was written by the Tin Pan Alley ... Author interview with Dick Holler, Oct. 6, 2016.

Studio owner Charles Fuller Hunt bought a celesta ... Author interview with studio manager Phyllis Crosby, Oct. 2, 2016.

Next, the Guardsmen were flown to New York City ... Author interview with Chris Nunley, Bill Balogh and Billy Taylor, Oct. 1, 2016.

"Phil was great in the studio ..." Author email exchange with John Burdett, Oct. 17, 2016, with followups.

Gernhard and the Schwartz Brothers had cooked up ... "Gernhard Inks 2 Acts on Laurie," *Billboard*, Dec. 21, 1967; "Sarasota Law Student a Show Biz Success: Snoopy and Royal Guardsmen to Hit Parade Peak," *Tampa Tribune*, Dec. 23, 1967.

"Phil tried to please us with the releases ..." Author email exchange with

John Burdett, Oct. 17, 2016.

"I think Schulz's people probably got on his ass ..." Author interview with Dick Holler, Oct. 6, 2016.

The Schulz-illustrated album jacket ... Author interview with Billy Taylor, Oct. 31, 2016.

The band embarked on a 10-city tour ... "Royal Guardsmen in Bid to Raise $500,000 for Needy Children," December 1967 newspaper clipping in the collection of Ed Tucker; International News Reports From the Music Capitals of the World, *Billboard*, Dec. 23, 1967.

"We are trying to develop a new industry in Florida ..." "Sarasota Law Student a Show Biz Success: Snoopy and Royal Guardsmen to Hit Parade Peak," *Tampa Tribune*, Dec. 23, 1967.

Chapter 7: Can You Tell Me Where He's Gone

"The way you produce a record is you hear a song ..." "The Middleman," the *Muezzin* (University of Tampa Alumni Magazine), May 1971.

Like the others on Gernhard's payroll ... Curtis, Kurt "K.O.T.O," *Florida's Famous & Forgotten: History of Florida's Rock, Soul & Dance Music, The First 30 Years 1955-1985*, Florida Media, Inc; "Sarasota Law Student a Show Biz Success: Snoopy and Red Baron Spin Royal Guardsmen to Hit Parade Peak," *Tampa Tribune*, Dec. 26, 1967 "Gernhard Inks 2 Acts on Laurie," *Billboard*, Dec. 21, 1967.

"Hey, getting a national record deal?" Author interview with William G. "Bill" Carson, Dec. 22, 2016.

His coffers still plentiful with Snoopy money ... Curtis, Kurt "K.O.T.O," *Florida's Famous & Forgotten: History of Florida's Rock, Soul & Dance Music, The First 30 Years 1955-1985*, Florida Media, Inc.

Gernhard Enterprises entered the concert promotion business ... "Sarasota Law Student a Show Biz Success: Snoopy and Royal Guardsmen to Hit Parade Peak," *Tampa Tribune*, Dec. 23, 1967.

Gernhard had had hired Ronny Elliott ... Author interview with Ronny

Elliott, Sept. 24, 2016, and email followups.

"Anybody like Joplin, who was making ten grand for one night's work ..." "Baby, I'm Gonna Make You a Star," *St. Petersburg Times*, Feb. 21, 1971.

Tensions were mounting in the Royal Guardsmen camp ... Author interview with Chris Nunley, Bill Balogh and Billy Taylor, Oct. 1, 2016.

In the spring of 1968, Winslow quit the band ... Author interview with Barry Winslow, Oct. 2, 2016, and email followups.

Meanwhile, the presidential primaries were in full swing ... Author interview with Dick Holler, Oct. 6, 2016.

With high school out of the way, the band was free ... Author interview with Billy Taylor, Oct. 31, 2016.

"I would imagine it would be simple to manage one person ..." Author email exchange with John Burdett, Oct. 17, 2016, with followups.

"By that time ..." Author interview with Billy Taylor, Oct. 31, 2016.

"We felt slighted, but relieved we didn't have to record ..." Author email exchange with John Burdett, Oct. 17, 2016, with followups.

Holler and Gernhard were in New York ... International News Reports From the Music Capitals of the World," *Billboard*, Feb. 17, 1968.

"It's a three or four-day project ..." Author interview with Dick Holler, Nov. 12, 2016.

"The real turning point for me was when I drove down to St. Pete ..." Author interview with Barry Winslow, Oct. 2, 2016.

Gernhard and Holler spent a month trying out singers ... Author interview with Dick Holler, Nov. 12, 2016.

Then Laurie boss Gene Schwartz asked Gernhard ... "Hot Producer P. Gernhard Singles Out New Single," *Billboard*, Dec. 21, 1968.

"He was doing all these folk songs for me ..." Writer Bob Frost's unpublished notes from a 2000 interview with Gernhard about "Abraham, Martin and John."

"I don't know why, but when I picked up a gut-string guitar and started putting it together ..." DiMucci, Dion, with Davin Seay, *The Wanderer: Dion's Story*, Beach Tree Books/William Morrow.

"I walk in the hall and there's Dion DiMucci ..." Author interview with Barry Winslow, Oct. 2, 2016.

Undaunted, Gernhard — with the full support of the Schwartz Brothers and Morris ... Writer Bob Frost's unpublished notes from a 2000 interview with Gernhard about "Abraham, Martin and John."

A DJ friend of Dick Holler's said the Dion single was *too* subtle ... Author interview with Dick Holler, Nov. 12, 2016.

Gernhard hung up the phone and put his head in his hands. Writer Bob Frost's unpublished notes from a 2000 interview with Gernhard about "Abraham, Martin and John."

"I don't want to brag ..." Author interview with Dick Holler, Nov. 12, 2016.

"We first heard this next song on the radio ... Transcription from CBS-TV, *The Smothers Brothers Comedy Hour*, Nov. 17, 1968.

At Gernhard's suggestion, DiMucci drew up a list ... DiMucci, Dion, with Davin Seay, *The Wanderer: Dion's Story*, Beach Tree Books/William Morrow.

Chapter 8: Someday Soon

"He could hand out the candy when he wanted something ..." Author interview with Barry Winslow, Oct. 2, 2016, and email followups.

"It was more than that he was full of himself ..." Author interview with Ronny Elliott, Sept. 24, 2016, and email followups.

"He was just throwing us a bone ..." Author interview with Chris Nunley, Bill Balogh and Billy Taylor, Oct. 1, 2016; Author interview with Billy Taylor, Oct. 31, 2016.

He and Holler dug Snoopy and the German out of the closet ... Author interview with Dick Holler, Oct. 6, 2016.

Elliott, meanwhile, knew how to push Gernhard's buttons. Author interview with Ronny Elliott, Sept. 24, 2016, and email followups.

Gernhard the entrepreneur cast his eye towards more civic matters ... "Beach Meeting Grows Heated," *St. Petersburg Evening Independent*, May 2, 1969. "Beach Backers to Amend Suit," *St. Petersburg Evening Independent*, Aug. 23, 1969. "Concession Hassle Continues," *St. Petersburg Evening Independent*, Jan. 24, 1970.

"That was all he needed to say to me ..." Author interview with Kent LaVoie, Nov. 22, 2016.

"I used to call myself a mercenary songwriter," Author interview with Kent LaVoie, Sept. 9, 2020.

In January 1970, Gernhard told ... "Gernhard Quits Rock Promotion," *St. Petersburg Evening Independent*, Feb. 10, 1970.

In February, the St. Petersburg Beach ... "Beach City Beer Facility Gets Approval," *St. Petersburg Times*, Feb. 18, 1970.

"I was about 14 when Phil gave me a ride home ..." Author email exchange with Ed Wright, Oct. 10, 2016.

In autumn 1970, Phil Gernhard booked ... Author interview with Ronny Elliott, Sept. 27, 2016, and email followups. "Bootleg Series #7: Derek and the Dominos Live at Curtis Hixon Hall, Tampa, FL USA 1st December 1970, www.tomcarswell.net.

Chapter 9: Introducing Lobo

As head of A&R for Laurie in the mid 1960s ... Doug Morris Interview, *Billboard*, Oct. 10. 2008. Doug Morris Midem Keynote Interview 2015, YouTube (video).

As a matter of fact, he did ... Author interview with Kent LaVoie, Nov. 22, 2016.

"Phil thought Kent had hit records in him ..." Author interview with Ronny Elliott, Sept. 24, 2016.

"We used my real name on 'Happy Days in New York City'..." Author interview with Kent LaVoie, Nov. 22, 2016; "2 Tampa-ites Group; Creates Lobo Hits," Creative Trends, *Billboard,* June 30, 1973.

Flush with Lobo cash ... Author interview with Ronny Elliott, Sept. 27, 2016, and email followups.

"It was Number One in *Cash Box* and *Record World* ..." Author interview with Kent LaVoie, Nov. 22, 2016.

"I was the first artist signed to the label ..." Author interview with Mike Curb, Oct. 20, 2016.

Ex-Royal Guardsman Barry Winslow was struggling ... Author interview with Ronny Elliott, Sept. 24, 2016; Author interview with Kent LaVoie, Nov. 22, 2016.

LaVoie remembers the day he received a phone call ... Author interview with Kent LaVoie, Nov. 22, 2016.

Stafford was booked at the Shack Upon the Beach ... Author interview with Jim Stafford, Dec. 19, 2016.

"We were drinking beer ..." Author interview with Kent LaVoie, Nov. 22, 2016.

"I worked at trying to figure out how to entertain people ..." Author interview with Jim Stafford, Dec. 19, 2016.

When Stafford played the little cassette demo ... Author interview with Kent LaVoie, Nov. 22, 2016.

"I think he saw potential in me not only ..." Author interview with Jim Stafford, Dec. 19, 2016.

Chapter 10: You Fool, You Fool

"Phil was one of the top ten producers that year ..." Author interview with Mike Curb, Oct. 20, 2016.

"'Swamp Witch' sold half a million copies ..." Author interview with Jim Stafford, Dec. 19, 2016.

"I wrote a novel called *The Mailman Cometh* ..." Author email exchange with Leo Gallagher, Oct. 13, 2016.

They were back in Venice ... Author interview with Jim Stafford, Dec. 19, 2016.

By 1973, the band was history ... "Interview with Howard Bellamy by Gary James," www.classicbands.com, date unknown.

"'I don't like spiders and snakes ..." Author interview with Jim Stafford, Dec. 19, 2016.

Growing up on a cattle ranch in a little town ... "Bellamys Happy to Stay Florida Boys," *Ft. Lauderdale Sun-Sentinel*, March 25, 2005; "Interview with Howard Bellamy by Gary James," www.classicbands.com, date unknown; *Country Music: The Encyclopedia*, Stambler, Irwin and Landon, Grelun. St. Martin's Griffin.

"Spiders and Snakes" became the first recording ... Author interview with Mike Curb, Oct. 20, 2016.

"When I got to Gernhard's office ..." David Bellamy, *Let Your Love Flow: The Life and Times of the Bellamy Brothers*, DarBella Publishing, LLC (April 13, 2018), page 102.

The success of this single corresponded with the end of Phil's marriage to Sandy... Author interview with Sandy Gernhard, Oct. 17, 2016.

New Jersey singer Tony Scotti ... Al Aronowitz, "The Dumb Sound," *Saturday Evening Post,* August 1963; "First and Goal: Former Players Tony & Ben Scotti, Looking to Score with the Redskins," *Washington Post*, Dec. 15, 1998.

"On their honeymoon, they went to see Jim Stafford ..." Author interview with Mike Curb, Nov. 21, 2016.

Although Gernhard-Scotti Enterprises wasn't registered ... "New Companies," *Billboard*, Feb. 22, 1975.

They leased three small white bungalows at 9229 Sunset Boulevard ... Author interview with Kent Lavoie, Nov. 22, 2016.

With her husband gone so much of the time ... Author interview with Sandy Gernhard, Oct. 10, 2016.

"I had a very physically and verbally abusive husband …" Author interview with Deborah Triplett, Oct. 26, 2016.

"He knew people …" Author interview with Kent Lavoie, Nov. 22, 2016.

The Bellamys took to calling him "Black Bart" … David Bellamy, *Let Your Love Flow: The Life and Times of the Bellamy Brothers*, DarBella Publishing, LLC (April 13, 2018), page 115.

"He never seemed to be happy with any women in his life …" Author interview with Jim Stafford, Dec. 19, 2016.

In the Hollywood Heights section of Los Angeles … Author email exchange with Leo Gallagher, Oct. 13, 2016; Author interview with Madeline Calder, Nov. 20, 2016.

Gernhard then became romantically involved … Author email exchange with Eve (Graham) Finn, Dec. 2, 2016, with followups.

Through Scotti's connections … Author interview with Dick Holler, Oct. 6, 2016.

"I started to fall in love with Phil because of …" Author interview with Deborah Triplett, Oct. 26, 2016, and email followups.

"After 'Swamp Witch,' this is when Phil …" Author interview with Kent Lavoie, Nov. 22, 2016.

Before things between them had gone south … Author interview with Kent Lavoie, Nov. 22, 2016; Author interview with Judee Gernhard, Nov. 11, 2016.

Chapter 11: Let Your Love Flow

"Looking back on it, it would've been nice if you'd had enough sense …" Author interview with Jim Stafford, Dec. 19, 2016.

After Stafford's "re-interpretation" of "Spiders and Snakes" … Author interview with Mike Curb, Oct. 20, 2016.

"I did that with a few songs …" Author interview with Jim Stafford, Dec. 19, 2016.

"The likeable Stafford easily outdoes ..." "Jim Stafford Aiming for Originality in New Series," *Chicago Tribune*, July 29, 1975.

"Phil was in his element when he was producing records ..." Author interview with Jim Stafford, Dec. 19, 2016.

Gernhard heard the song's potential immediately. Author interview with Mike Curb, Oct. 20, 2016.

"Tony and I were standing there talking ..." *The Billboard Book of Number One Hits*, Fred Bronson, Billboard Publications.

"Phil would rub the top of his moustache ..." Author interview with Mike Curb, Oct. 20, 2016.

"Howard was on the road with me for a long time ..." sense ..." Author interview with Jim Stafford, Dec. 19, 2016.

Gernhard told an interviewer he'd received letters ... *The Billboard Book of Number One Hits*, Fred Bronson, Billboard Publications.

"Phil's production on that record ..." Author interview with Mike Curb, Oct. 20, 2016.

"I don't know what the deal was that the Scottis cut with Phil ..." Author interview with Jim Stafford, Dec. 19, 2016.

"Phil was doing all the production ..." Author interview with Deborah Triplett, Oct. 26, 2016, and email followups.

"That sold a couple of million records, and Phil suggested ..." "The Bellamys gain a British following," *Country Music People*, November 1979.

At home in Florida, Kent LaVoie got a copy ... Author interview with Kent LaVoie, Nov. 22, 2016.

"The heater was in my part, so I could hear Jim and Madeline argue ..." Author email exchange with Leo Gallagher, Oct. 13, 2016.

"If success just slugs you, I think that you don't always behave good ..." Author interview with Jim Stafford, Dec. 19, 2016.

"Gernhard had power of attorney over us ... David Bellamy, *Let Your Love Flow: The Life and Times of the Bellamy Brothers*, DarBella Publishing, LLC

(April 13, 2018), page 139.

"Phil did the second album, but then he turned it over to Michael Lloyd ..." Author interview with Mike Curb, Oct. 20, 2016.

"He *made* the Bellamy Brothers ..." Author interview with Deborah Triplett, Oct. 26, 2016.

"I think it was common with him and the bunch ..." Author interview with Jim Stafford, Dec. 19, 2016.

Jim Stafford, Phil Gernhard and Tony Scotti acknowledge ... paid advertisement in *Billboard*, Feb. 19, 1977.

"Phil was very Hollywood ..." Author interview with Kent Lavoie, Nov. 22, 2016.

While he was away playing politics in Sacramento ... Author interview with Mike Curb, Nov. 21, 2016.

For a while, Stafford remained Phil's primary ... "Jim Stafford: Southern comfort, Vegas-style," *St. Petersburg Times*, Jan. 22, 1978.

"I think it would be fairly safe to say ..." Author interview with Jim Stafford, Dec. 19, 2016.

Chapter 12: Lookin' for a Hit

"Phil was like a different guy in the studio ..." Author interview with James House, Jan. 11, 2018.

Gernhard went to Curb president Whitehouse ... Author interview with Mike Curb, Oct. 20, 2016; Author interview with Don Dixon, Dec. 12, 2016.

"We were caught between being a coliseum rock act ..." Author interview with Don Dixon, Dec. 12, 2016.

"I had to go pick up something from his hotel room ..." Author interview with Don Dixon, Dec. 12, 2016.

After a five-year courtship ... "Down in Front," *St. Petersburg Evening Independent*, Nov. 20, 1980.

By then, she'd had a drunken earful ... Author interview with Deborah

Triplett, Oct. 26, 2016, and email followups.

The sessions took place at Electric Lady ... "Electric Lady Negligence Suit, *Billboard*, Oct. 18, 1980.

This settlement in hand, Gernhard block-booked Alpha Audio in downtown Richmond ... Author interview with Chuck Larson, Nov. 7, 2016, and email followups.

"Phil never had friends, and that ..." Author interview with Deborah Triplett, Oct. 26, 2016, and email followups.

Chapter 13: You Either Drag or You Get Drug

"We talked a lot after he moved to Nashville ..." Author interview with Deborah Triplett, Oct. 26, 2016.

"There was no life except work for a while there ..." "Music Man: Phil Gernhard Has Ear For Music and Eye For the Right Artist," *Sarasota Herald-Tribune*, Sept. 3, 1988.

"He was raving about the record we'd done ..." Author interview with Byron Gallimore, Dec. 8, 2016.

"From my perspective, I give him total credit for breaking Tim ..." Author interview with Byron Gallimore, Dec. 8, 2016.

"He didn't sign Tim McGraw, but he played ..." Author interview with Mike Curb, Oct. 20, 2016.

"We made fast friends ..." Author interview with Byron Gallimore, Dec. 8, 2016.

Sara Arnold Gernhard died in a Sarasota nursing home ... Author interview with Judee Gernhard, Oct. 13, 2016; Author interview with Sandy Gernhard, Oct. 17, 2016.

"Phil's expectations of his wives was that they would be perfect ..." Author interview with Mike Curb, Oct. 20, 2016.

"I remember on the night he got married to Pat ..." Author interview with Mike Curb, Oct. 20, 2016.

In February, during her engagement to Gernhard ... *Dateline NBC: Through the Pouring Rain*, aired 10-9-09.

"Phil was an incredibly difficult person ..." Author interview with Pat Young, Nov. 21, 2016.

" ... they got divorced primarily ... Author interview with Mike Curb, Oct. 20, 2016.

Young would only say ... Author interview with Pat Young, Nov. 21, 2016.

When Gallimore and McGraw introduced her to Gernhard ... RolandNote. com; the Ultimate Country Music Database.

"He understood the relationship between promotion and creativity ..." Author interview with Mike Curb, Nov. 21, 2016.

At his suggestion, Missi got back into ... Author interview with Kelly Lynn, Nov. 17, 2016.

Alone in his big empty house, Gernhard sometimes called ... Author interview with Sandy Gernhard, Oct. 10, 2016; Author interview with Deborah Triplett, Oct. 26, 2016, and email followups.

"I hated going home after my mother was gone ..." Author interview with Judee Gernhard, Nov. 11, 2016.

Chapter 14: If You're Going Through Hell

"At the time, I didn't know his background ..." Author interview with Byron Gallimore, Dec. 1, 2016.

"I've heard people say that Phil was so blunt ..." Author interview with Rodney Atkins, Jan. 30, 2017.

"I can make it real simple ..." Author interview with Mike Curb, Oct. 20, 2016.

It was the addictions, Curb figured ... Author interview with Mike Curb, Nov. 21, 2016.

A six-song demo CD from a teenage Swedish singer ... Author interview with Mike Curb, Nov. 21, 2016; "Number One With a Bullet" by P.J. Tobia, *Nashville Scene*, September 2008.

Meet Sofia Loell, a Scandinavian import ... Singles, *Billboard*, May 25, 2003.

Gernhard traveled to Stockholm that fall ... "Number One With a Bullet" by P.J. Tobia, *Nashville Scene*, September 2008.

Just after Christmas, back in Nashville ... Author interview with Byron Gallimore, Dec. 1, 2016.

Curb never met the fourth Mrs. Gernhard ... Author interview with Mike Curb, Nov. 21, 2016.

He told his friends he was putting her through school ... Author interview with Judee Gernhard, Nov. 11, 2016.

"From the minute I met Phil ..." Author interview with Kelly Lynn, Nov. 17, 2016.

There wasn't much enthusiasm in the air ... Author interview with Rodney Atkins, Jan. 30, 2017.

Immediately, Kelly brought her to Phil Gernhard. Author interview with Ashley Gearing, Dec. 12, 2016.

"In all the years we worked together ..." Author interview with Byron Gallimore, Dec. 8, 2016.

"I knew he'd had a lot of pain in his lifetime ..." Author interview with Ashley Gearing, Dec. 12, 2016.

"You're bringing Phil Gernhard back to life ..." Author interview with Ashley Gearing, Dec. 12, 2016.

"I know he had a lot of doctor's appointments ..." Author interview with Kelly Lynn, Nov. 17, 2016.

Gearing watched him struggle ... Author interview with Ashley Gearing, Dec. 12, 2016.

"Phil would call me, or my daughter in Texas ..." Author interview with Judee Gernhard, Oct. 13, 2016.

She was also known as "Madeline Hamilton," ... "Number One With a Bullet" by P.J. Tobia, *Nashville Scene*, September 2008; www.madeline-stockholmescort.com.

"He was devastated ..." Author interview with Judee Gernhard, Oct. 13, 2016.

"I'll bet he did know ..." Author interview with Kelly Lynn, Nov. 17, 2016.

Ashley Gearing dropped by with Kelly ... Author interview with Ashley Gearing, Dec. 12, 2016;

When the hibachi chef produced a sudden wall of flame ... Author interview with Ashley Gearing, Dec. 12, 2016; email followup with with Kelly Lynn.

"If my friend, Elizabeth Vernon ..." Last Will and Testament of Philip Arnold Gernhard, Davidson County probate court, revision signed 7-13-07.

Five days later, he filed ... Complaint for Divorce, Philip Arnold Gernhard vs. Anna Maria Pettersson, Fourth Circuit Court, Davidson County, Tennessee, filed 7-18-07, and followup documents.

Chapter 15:w A Safe Place

"A lot of people at the label at the time thought it was too risky ...." Author interview with Rodney Atkins, Jan. 30, 2017.

"Phil was saying to me 'Oh, if I could just get one more No. 1...." Author interview with Mike Curb, Nov. 21, 2016.

Through their lawyers, he and Maria finally agreed on terms ... Complaint for Divorce, Philip Arnold Gernhard vs. Anna Maria Pettersson, Fourth Circuit Court, Davidson County, Tennessee, filed 7-18-07, and followup documents.

As was his custom, Gernhard spent Christmas Day ... Author interview with Mike Curb, Nov. 21, 2016.

On New Year's Eve, Metro Police stopped ... Nashville Metropolitan Police Department Incident Report dated 12-31-07.

"The one thing that bothered me..." Author interview with Ashley Gearing, Dec. 12, 2016.

"Phil was always the guy who called me …" Author interview with Mike Curb, Nov. 21, 2016.

"He told me he was proud of me…" Author interview with Rodney Atkins, Jan. 30, 2017.

On Tuesday morning, Phil and Kelly met on schedule at the Waffle House … Author interview with Kelly Lynn, Nov. 17, 2016.

By Friday, the 22nd, he hadn't returned calls, from anyone. Author interview with Kelly Lynn, Nov. 17, 2016; Author interview with Mike Curb, Nov. 21, 2016.

At lunchtime, Kelly drove over to the Brentwood house. Author interview with Kelly Lynn, Nov. 17, 2016.

Just before 1 p.m., after their entreaties met only silence … Nashville Metropolitan Police Department Incident Report dated 2-22-08.

"I'll never forget the minute I walked out of my son's school …" Author interview with Kelly Lynn, Nov. 17, 2016.

"If you look at the pad of paper he had …" Author interview with Mike Curb, Oct. 20, 2016.

Because the circumstances of his death … Tennessee Dept. of Health and Enviroment Medical Examiner's Report, dated 2-23-08.

"The thing that beat me up about it," reflected Rodney Atkins … Author interview with Rodney Atkins, Jan. 30, 2017.

Steve Parker, Phil's executor … Author interview with Betty Vernon, Oct. 2, 2016.

"At that point, I didn't know anybody at Curb …" Author interview with Ashley Gearing, Dec. 12, 2016.

The September 18 edition of *Nashville Scene* … "Number One With a Bullet" by P.J. Tobia, *Nashville Scene*, September 2008.

"What I wish I'd said to him was: 'Phil, I'm not here for …" Author interview with Kent Lavoie, Nov. 22, 2016.

Ten, twenty, thirty, forty, fifty or more!

PRODUCTIONS BY PHIL GERNHARD

Singles Discography

For years marked *, production on all titles credited to Briarwood Enterprises (Phil Gernhard/Johnny McCullough)

1959

Cole 100 Maurice Williams and the Zodiacs, "Golly Gee" / "'T' Town" (no producer listed on label)

Cole 101 Maurice Williams and the Zodiacs, "Lover (Where Are You?)" / "She's Mine" ("A P. Gernhard and J. Turner Production" on label)

1960*

Herald 552 Maurice Williams and the Zodiacs, "Stay" / "Do You Believe"

Herald 556 Maurice Williams and the Zodiacs, "I Remember" / "Always"

1961*

Herald 559 Maurice Williams and the Zodiacs, "Come Along" / "Do I"

Herald 563 Maurice Williams and the Zodiacs, "Come and Get It" / "Some Day"

May MY 104 Clark Summit, "Holding Hands" / "Why Not"

Herald 564 Dale and the Del-Hearts, "I've Waited So Long" / "Always and Ever"

Madison 163 Jimmy Rand, "The Only Girl in My Life" / "Peggy, Peggy"

Rust 5036 The Monograms, "Baby Blue Eyes" / "Little Suzie"

Herald 565 Maurice Williams and the Zodiacs, "High Blood Pressure" / "Please"

Herald 566 Dick Holler and the Holidays, "King Kong" / "The Girl Next Door"

1962*

Herald 572 Maurice Williams and the Zodiacs, "It's Alright" / "Here I Stand"

Herald 575 Julie Gibson and the Anglows, "I Got News For You" / "You've Been Cheatin' On Me" (B-side by "The Angloes Featuring Barbara")

Comet 2146 Dick Holler and the Holidays, "Mooba Grooba" / "Hey Little Fool"

Comet 2152 Dick Holler and the Holidays, "(Double Shot) Of My Baby's Love" / "Yea-Boo"

Fire 512 Linda Martell and the Anglos, "A Little Tear (Was Falling from My Eyes)" / "The Things I Do For You"

1963*

Laurie 3207 The Archers, "Hey Rube" / "Unwind It" 1965

Knight 101 The Sugar Beats, "What Am I Doing Here" / "Have You Ever Had the Blues"

Knight 102 The Tropics, "I Want More" / "Goodbye My Love" 1966

Knight 103 The Outsiders, "Just Let Me Be" / "She's Coming on Stronger"

Laurie 3330 The Tropics, "You Better Move" / "It's You I'll Miss"

Knight 104 The Outsiders, "Summertime Blues" / "Set You Free This Time"

Providence 414 The Soul Trippers, "King Bee" / "Girl of Mine"

Laurie 3350 Royal Guardsmen, "Baby Let's Wait" / "Leaving Me"

Laurie 3366X (Canada) Royal Guardsmen, "Squeaky vs. the Black Knight" / "I Needed You" Laurie 3366

Laurie 3336 Royal Guardsmen, "Snoopy vs. the Red Baron" / "I Needed You"

1967

Laurie 3379 Royal Guardsmen, "The Return of the Red Baron" / "Sweetmeats Slide"

Laurie 3391 Royal Guardsmen, "Airplane Song (My Airplane)" / "Om"

Decca 32205 The Dream Machine, "Houdini" / "Broken Hearts"

Laurie 3397 Royal Guardsmen, "Any Wednesday" / "So Right (To Be in Love)"

Laurie 3416 Royal Guardsmen, "Snoopy's Christmas" / "It Kinda Looks Like Christmas"

1968

Laurie 3411 Hoppi and the Beau Heems, "I Missed My Cloud" / "So Hard"

Laurie 3428 Royal Guardsmen, "I Say Love" / "I'm Not Gonna Stay"

Rust 5123 The Raven, "Calamity Jane" / "Now She's Gone"

Laurie 3439 Hoppi and the Beau Heems, "When I Get Home" / "So Hard"

Laurie 3451 Royal Guardsmen, "Snoopy For President" / "Down Behind the Lines"

Laurie 3461 Royal Guardsmen, "Baby Let's Wait" / "So Right (To Be in Love)"

Laurie 3464 Dion, "Abraham, Martin and John" / "Daddy Rollin' (In Your Arms)"

1969

Laurie 3478 Dion, "Purple Haze" / "The Dolphins"

Laurie 3487 Dick Holler, "Amos-Ben-Haren-Hab-Seti-14" / "Sylvia"

Laurie 3491 GAP, "Sheriff" / "Theme From The Sheriff"

Laurie 3494 Royal Guardsmen, "Mother Where's Your Daughter" / "Magic Window"

Laurie 3495 Dion, "From Both Sides Now" / "Sun Fun Song"

Laurie 3509 Barry Winslow, "The Smallest Astronaut (A Race to the Moon with the Red Baron)" / "Quality Woman"

Laurie 3526 Kent LaVoie, "Happy Days in New York City" / "My Friend is Here"

Bell 870 M.O.U.S.E., "Where's the Little Girl" / "Knock on My Door"

1970

Warner Bros. 7401 Dion, "Your Own Back Yard" / "Sit Down, Old Friend"

Warner Bros. 7418 Chair, "Greater Miami Subterranean Rock Revival" / "Ride That American Dream"

Bell 918 M.O.U.S.E., "Woman or a Girl" / "I Can Only Touch You with My Eyes"

1971

Warner Bros. 7469 Dion, "Let It Be" / "Close To it All"

Paramount 0099 Duckbutter, "Gospel Trip (Medley)" / "Mountain Dream Song"

Big Tree 112 Lobo, "Me and You and a Dog Named Boo" / "Walk Away

From it All"

Warner Bros. 7491 Dion, "Sunniland" / "Josie"

Big Tree 116 Lobo, "She Didn't Do Magic" / "I'm the Only One"

Big Tree 119 Lobo, "California Kid and Reemo" / "A Little Different"

1972

Big Tree 132 Israel, "Captain America" / "You'd Better Move On"

Big Tree 134 Lobo, "The Albatross" / "We'll Make It--I Know We Will"

Big Tree 141 Lobo, "A Simple Man" / "Don't Expect Me to Be Your Friend"

Big Tree 147 Lobo, "I'd Love You to Want Me" / "Am I True to Myself"

Big Tree 158 Lobo, "Don't Expect Me to Be Your Friend" / "A Big Red Kite"

1973

Warner Bros. 7537 Dion, "Sanctuary" / "Brand New Morning"

Big Tree 16000 Barry Winslow, "Get to Know Me" / "Where There's Love There's Fire"

Big Tree 16001 Lobo, "It Sure Took a Long, Long Time" / "Running Deer"

Big Tree 16004 Lobo, "How Can I Tell Her" / "Hope You're Proud of Me Girl"

MGM 14496 Jim Stafford, "Swamp Witch" / "Nifty Fifties Blues" (coproduced with Lobo)

Warner Bros. 7704 Dion, "Doctor Rock and Roll" / "Sunshine Lady"

Big Tree 16012 Lobo, "There Ain't No Way" / "Love Me For What I Am" 1974

MGM 14718 Jim Stafford, "My Girl Bill" / "L.A. Mamma" (coproduced with Lobo)

MGM 14737 Jim Stafford, "Wildwood Weed" / "The Last Chant" (coproduced with Lobo)

Big Tree 15001 Lobo, "Stoney" / "Standing at the End of the Line"

ABC Dunhill 15007 Petula Clark, "Never Been a Horse That Couldn't Be Rode" / "I'm the Woman You Need" (coproduced with Tony Scotti)

MGM 14648 Jim Stafford, "Spiders & Snakes" / "Undecided" (coproduced with Lobo)

Big Tree 15008 Lobo, "Rings" / "I'm Only Sleeping"

ABC Dunhill 15019 Petula Clark, "Loving Arms" / "I'm the Woman You Need" (coproduced with Tony Scotti)

MGM 14775 Jim Stafford, "Your Bulldog Drinks Champagne" / "A Real Good Time" (coproduced with Lobo)

Polydor 2058 519 (UK only) Petula Clark, "Let's Sing a Love Song" / "I'm the Woman You Need" (coproduced with Tony Scotti)

1975

MGM 14859 Jim Stafford, "I Got Stoned and I Missed It" / "I Ain't Working" (coproduced with Lobo)

Big Tree 16033 Lobo, "Don't Tell Me Goodnight" / "My Momma Had Soul"

Warner/Curb 8123 David Bellamy, "Nothin' Heavy" / "Baby, You're Not a Legend" (coproduced with Tony Scotti)

Warner/Curb 8136 Chuck Conlon, "Mighty Lighty Moon" / "Wish I Could Have Told You" (coproduced with Tony Scotti)

Warner/Curb 8169 Bellamy Brothers, "Let Your Love Flow" / "Inside of My Guitar" (coproduced with Tony Scotti)

Big Tree 16040 Lobo, "Would I Still Have You" / "Morning Sun"

Warner/Curb 8271 Deborah Allen, "Do You Copy" / "Take Me Back" (coproduced with Jim Stafford)

1976

Warner/Curb 8248 Bellamy Brothers, "Satin Sheets" / "Rainy, Windy, Sunshine (Rodeo Road)" (coproduced with Tony Scotti)

Polydor 14309 Jim Stafford, "Jasper" / "I Can't Find Nobody Home"

Warner/Curb 8284 Bellamy Brothers, "Highway 2-18 (Hang On to Your Dreams)" / "Livin' in the West"

1977

Warner / Curb 8299 Jim Stafford, "Turn Loose of My Leg" / "The Flight" (coproduced with Tony Scotti)

Warner/Curb 8350 Bellamy Brothers, "Crossfire" / "Tiger Lily Lover"

Warner/Curb 8401 Bellamy Brothers, "You Made Me" / "Can Somebody Hear Me Now"

Warner/Curb 8462 Bellamy Brothers, "Memorabilia" / "Hard Rockin'"

Warner/Curb 8538 Jim Stafford, "You Can Call Me Clyde" / "One Step Ahead of the Law"

1978

Warner/Curb 8493 Lobo, "Afterglow" / "Our Best Time"

Warner/Curb 8537 Lobo, "You Are All I'll Ever Need" / "Our Best Time"

Warner/Curb 8564 Hank Williams Jr., "You Love the Thunder" / "I Just Ain't Been Able"

Warner/Curb 8601 Prisoner, "Fool (If You Think It's Over)"

Warner/Curb 8635 Prisoner, "Hot Summer Night/ / I Wanna Be the One"

Warner/Curb 8702 Prisoner, "Try a Little Tenderness / I Wanna Be the One"

1979

Warner/Curb 49079 Bobby Hart, "The Loneliest Night" / "Sometimes Love" (coproduced with Bobby Hart and Barry Richards)

Warner/Curb 49044 Arrogance, "Secrets" / "Your Sister Told Me" (coproduced with Michael Lloyd)

1980

Warner/Curb 49152 Arrogance, "It Ain't Cool to Be Cruel" / "What's Done Is Done"

Warner/Curb 49232 Arrogance, "What It Takes" / "Burning Desire"

1981

Elektra E-47226 Jim Stafford, "Isabel and Samantha" / "Yeller Dog Blues" 1982

Elektra/Curb 69897 Snuff, "When Jokers Are Wild" / "Heaven in Your Eyes" 1983

Warner/Curb 29615 Snuff, "Bad, Bad Billy" / "Defiance"

Albums Discography

1961

Herald HLP 1014 Maurice Williams and the Zodiacs (co-produced with Johnny McCullough, as Briarwood Enterprises), Stay

1966

Laurie SLP 2038 The Royal Guardsmen, Snoopy vs. the Red Baron

1967

Laurie SLP 2039 The Royal Guardsmen, The Return of the Red Baron

Laurie SLLP 2042 The Royal Guardsmen, Snoopy and His Friends

1968

Laurie SLP 2046 The Royal Guardsmen, Snoopy for President

Laurie SLP 2047 Dion, "Dion"

1970

Atlantic SD 8268 Dick Holler, Someday Soon

Warner Bros. WBS 1826 Dion, Sit Down Old Friend

1971

Big Tree BTS 2003 Lobo, Introducing Lobo

Warner Bros. WS 1872 Dion, You're Not Alone

1972

Big Tree BT 2013 Lobo, Of a Simple Man

1973

Big Tree BT 2101 Lobo, Calumet

1974

MGM SE 4947 Jim Stafford (co-produced with Lobo), "Jim Stafford"

Big Tree BT 89501 Lobo, Just a Singer

1975

MGM MG3-4984 Jim Stafford (co-produced with Lobo), Not Just Another Pretty Foot

Big Tree BT 89505 Lobo, A Cowboy Afraid of Horses

1976

Warner/Curb BS 2941 Bellamy Brothers, Bellamy Brothers (Featuring "Let Your Love Flow" and Others) (co-produced with Tony Scotti)

1977

Warner/Curb BS 3034 Bellamy Brothers, Plain & Fancy

1980

Warner/Curb 3429 Arrogance, Suddenly

1982

Elektra/Curb 60149 Snuff, Snuff

1983

Warner/Curb 23910 Snuff, Night Fighter (EP)

The author gratefully acknowledges the record-collecting websites discogs.com, 45cat.com, and popsike.com, along with Kurt "K.O.T.O." Curtis's book *Florida's Famous & Forgotten: An Illustrated Encyclopedia History of Florida's Rock, Soul & Dance Music, the First 30 Years: 1955-1985* (Florida Media, 2005).

About the author

The author with Jim Stafford, Jan. 6, 2018.

Born and raised in St. Petersburg, Bill DeYoung was a music fan from an early age. Although he never met Phil Gernhard, he knew his name, and his legacy, and was always aware of the contributions he'd made to the Florida music industry.

Other books by Bill DeYoung: Skyway: *The True Story of Tampa Bay's Signature Bridge and the Man Who Brought it Down* (University Press of Florida), and *I Need to Know: The Lost Music Interviews* (St. Petersburg Press). He is also the author of three volumes of *Vintage St. Pete* stories (St. Petersburg Press).

www.ingramcontent.com/pod-product-compliance
Lightning Source LLC
Chambersburg PA
CBHW071322120626
46546CB00002B/397